Instructions From The Father

By: Nancy A Connell

Scripture taken from the Holy Bible, NEW INTERNATIONAL VERSION®, NIV® Copyright © 1973, 1978, 1984, 2011 by Biblica, Inc.® Used by permission. All rights reserved worldwide.

NEW INTERNATIONAL VERSION® and NIV® are registered trademarks of Biblica, Inc. Use of either trademark for the offering of goods or services requires the prior written consent of Biblica US, Inc.

ISBN: 978-0-9861572-2-6

Contact Author: shiningyourglory@gmx.com

For more prophetic words by other prophets and to be fed fresh manna from Heaven and to grow deeper in your walk with God visit:
Lighthousechurchinc.org

Check out some other books with spiritual food for your soul available in ebook or paperback:
Author: Brett Connell
A Remembrance [2015]   ISBN: 9780986157202
Heavens Courts [2016]   ISBN: 9780997454109

CONTENTS

SPECIAL THANKS

This book completely goes to the honor of God my Father, Jesus Christ my Savior, and the Holy Spirit, my best friend. Without the Holy Trinity this would not of taken place. I am only a bondservant that am willing to open my ears to hear His voice and to write down what He wants His children to know and to be obedient to His Will.

I want to thank Evangelist Pastor Barbara Lynch for guiding me and encouraging me to listen for God's voice. Thank you for teaching God's Word and the importance of walking holy and being obedient to God at all times. Thank you for always sticking with the truth and being a living example of what Christ is like no matter what. Thank you for encouraging me to keep going and correcting me when I was wrong. Thank you for your love and your prayers every step of the way.

I want to thank my husband, Brett Connell and our 8 beautiful children for all your support and encouragement. I am truly blessed to have you all in my life. Thank you for understanding and giving me time to sit in our Father's presence so that I could listen to His voice. Brett, thank you for all you do. Your support means a lot to me and thank you for loving me and walking with me in this journey God has called us into.

I want to thank Rev. Christopher Gore for encouraging me to let loose and let God have complete control in the process of learning and being confident that I know and hear God's voice and for your support.

And a thank you to all my family and friends who have supported my walk with God and I pray many blessings and great favor upon you all. I truly believe many lives will be touch and that God's Glory shall be spread through each word He has spoken.

INTRODUCTION

Please read it as God directs you to. You can read it straight through or go by what title God impresses on your heart to read for that day or the days to come. As you follow the instructions that He has given in this book you will find yourself walking closer to God than you ever had before. But realize they are only words on a paper unless you do apply them to your life.

There is many tools and nuggets that God has given in His instructions, and I pray that it plants seeds into your soul that will grow good fruit and will flourish in your lives and in the lives of others. I pray that many souls will be saved and lives changed to the Glory of God and encounters of a deeper walk with God is obtained.

I encourage you to check out the website lighthousechurchinc.org to have access to other Words given on a daily bases and to also be feed sermons and fresh manna from Heaven as God reveals to His people His plan and purpose for your lives.

Enjoy!

PERSONAL PRAYER

God I give you all praise, honor, and glory for all you are going to do with this book you have called together.

Thank you Heavenly Father for bring forth Your messages to your people. I love You, God with all my heart, body, and soul.

I ask you Holy Spirit to rest upon the person who reads this book. May the anointing flow and your presence be amplfied by the reading of your personal words to your people.

I am asking you Father with every person who reads this book open their hearts to receive what you have to say, eyes to see the truth, ears to hear additional things that you have to say, and a life that is changed and rearranged by the encounter of your Holy Spirit as He rests upon them.

May the blood of Jesus Christ cover each Word you have spoken and protect them from any attack from the enemy.

I ask of this in Jesus' name AMEN

PRAISE

Praise Me today. In absolutely everything, praise Me. As you praise Me throughout the day, you will feel My presence and My anointing. Do not stop praising Me because of a circumstance or something happens you do not like. Simply put it in My hands and praise Me.

I am transforming minds and hearts. As you praise Me, it opens the mind and heart so I can begin My work. You will be able to see the difference in your day as you focus on Me and just praise Me.

Have your children praise Me. Many people sing songs with their children off the radio or television so why not sing My praises with them? As you do this thing, I can begin to do the transformation in them as well.

JUST PRAISE ME!!!!

Psalms 33
****

PRAISE THROUGH EVERYTHING

My children do not understand the work that I am trying to do. I was only able start a work in a small few. Today praise Me. Be a living example of praise.

In praising Me comes your breakthrough. It is your break through from sin, from bondage, from discontentment, from discouragement, from depression, and the list goes on and on with what praising Me will do. As you praise Me it breaks down the walls from your mind, from your heart, from your life, and from your walk with Me.

It is the key to your freedom. It is the answer to your promise land that I have for you. The enemy has you build these walls to prevent Me from being able to have complete control to do My will and to set My children completely free. Do not hold onto Egypt.

When I released My children from Egypt, they were contented, happy, and encouraged as they praised Me. The moment they stopped praising is when they started complaining, their eyes were no longer focused on Me, their lives became a struggle, and no matter what I did for them, it was not enough.

They were not satisfied with the miracles that I performed for them. They took their eyes off of Me by not praising Me anymore, and they ended up losing out on what I promised them. Their minds and their hearts became clouded and corrupted because they quit praising Me.

As My children do praise Me, their minds and their hearts will stay focused on Me, and their faith will be at their fullest. The minds are more open to receive what I am trying to do and give.

Why do you think the enemy fights you and My children so hard in this area? If you are complaining, I cannot do My will in your life. It ties My hands. Complaining is what causes curses and speaks things into existence that I did not ordain to happen. I cannot bless those who are not grateful for the things that I do for them.

As My servant Paul praised Me, it left his heart open for Me to use him to help My people, to guide My people, and to give My people an example that it does not matter where you are or what is going on, as you praise Me, the situation will not affect you.

One of My tools of protection is praise. As My children praise Me in their prison of bondage, I can then set them free. I can then perform the miracles in their lives because their eyes will not be on their prison and bondage anymore, but on Me.

Great darkness is coming. There is not much time for My people to learn the tools to survive. Praise will break through the darkness. Do not be like My children that I freed from Egypt who became bound again by complaining and taking their eyes off of Me.

If you cannot learn to praise Me now, how are you going to praise Me when the darkness thickens? My people MUST praise Me through it all.

Try it My little ones. When you feel sad, angry, upset, alone, ... start praising Me. You will see the problems won't seem so big. The feelings of the darkness will go away, and you will begin to understand the strength in praise.

As you praise Me, My joy takes root and starts to bubble out of you. And it is with the joy that comes from praise that strengthens you. That is why satan tries to steal your joy and to prevent you from truly praising Me. It is in your praise that you can claim the victory over the problems and over the enemy because your focus is on Me.

So today My little ones, praise Me. When you are getting frustrated, praise Me. If the enemy tries to play with your mind in any way, praise Me.

I began the works on My children's minds and hearts on those that has begun to praise Me. It must continue to be a daily thing. Rise up higher than the ones before you, and watch My glory over take you.

The darkness will not have any effect on you. My praise will brighten your light. You will continue to watch Me work as you praise Me throughout the day. Make a vow to Me to daily praise Me and see what I will do for My people.

Psalm 33
****

MIND OF UNITY

Today My children, I am calling you to have a mind of unity. I desire you to let go of those things that so easily besets you. Let go of your own opinion, your own understanding, and your sin nature.

As you put your mind on Me, focus on Me, praise Me, unity can begin because you will desire My will. You will see My miracles begin to work.

I am calling you today to have a heart of compassion and humility. How can you open your arms to the hurt, dying, and lost souls without being a servant full of love?

I need you to let go of the bitterness, anger, and negative way of thinking. It is not your job to judge, but to love. For as you allow My love to flow through you. I can bring in those who I desire to save.

To do these things you need to have joy in your heart and your mind in unity with My Spirit. To do this you must praise Me continuously.

If you cannot find anything to praise Me for, I tell you just praise Me because I gave My Son to die for you and to be risen up to allow you to come to Heaven and be with Me. Praise Me for the life that has been given to you through salvation.

Grasp this tool of praise. Put it to use because I desire to teach you so much more. I need you to learn these tools so I can get you into the supernatural realm. It is in My supernatural realm that will keep you from the darkness that is quickly approaching.

There is no time to procrastinate or drag your feet or doubt My ways. Give Me your mind and your heart this day. Let Me do the works that I need to do in order to prepare you for all the knowledge that you will need to survive in Me.

My full glory is coming. My miracles, signs, and wonders are here. But I need you to learn how to get yourselves individually prepared to receive and to be willing to be worked through for My honor and glory.

Unity, humbleness, compassion, love, joy, and praise this is what I desire from you this day. Give up your mindsets and put on Mine. Stay focus on Me and stay in My presence and under My anointing and just see what I do as you enter this supernatural realm and with all My glory.

1 Peter 1:3; 1 Peter 3:8; 1 Peter 1:8
****

BUILD YOUR FAITH FOR THE SUPERNATURAL

As you have been praising Me, My children, a new thing has begun inside of you. As you learn to work together and love one another, as you are willing to serve Me with a grateful heart, as you learn to be joyous no matter what is going on around you, you will step into a new realm in Me.

Many of you desire the supernatural. Many of you want the signs, wonders, and miracles, but you lack the use of one of the greatest survival tools which is faith.

To be able to move into this new realm and tap into the supernatural you must strengthen your faith and trust in Me. You need blind faith. You need to know that with every fiber in your being that I will provide, protect, teach, and bring forth My promises.

There is no room for doubt. Doubt is like poison to the heart and the mind. It is like a wild vine that will take root and grow wild and eventually choke your spiritual life out of you. If you walk in unbelief that I can't do things for you, how can I openly do that of what I have promised to you? What would that teach you?

It would not build your faith at all. It would leave you wondering, my God did it for me this time, but I am not so sure He will do it next time. What kind of testimony would that be to My people? Yes, I allow different circumstances to happen to build your faith.

As I build your faith, you will let down and let go of your limitations on Me. When you allow the limitations to be broken and come down, it allows Me to begin the supernatural and do the great works on you that still needs to be done. I cannot express enough to you My children on how much I really need you to move forward in this supernatural realm.

Time is so short. I want you to enjoy serving Me. I want you to desire to walk with Me daily, to bring in My harvest of souls, and to just believe that what I say I will do.

14

Today I want you to walk in complete faith. I want you to give Me all control of absolutely everything. Put everything in My hands. Just rest in My peace and know that all is done taken care of. See how free you feel from all the burdens that you carry that is far from necessary. Have faith in Me that in the correct timing all that I have promised will surely come to pass.

Romans 4:20-21

****

COMPLETELY DEDICATE YOURSELF TO ME

My children, I have called you to walk in praise, in faith, in love, in humility, but you still find it difficult to do these simple tasks that I have asked. Why is this so? Your minds are corrupted by the world and of worldly things. You do not focus on Me at all times. The most times I hear from My children is when I am the last one they come to.

My children you must wake up. Time is so short. Time is not something to be wasted.

I need your minds, your hearts, and your wills. I need you by faith to know that I will be able to transform these things to make them pure and holy. I will transform your mind, your heart, and your soul to be able to do My work and walk My path and to have a very close relationship with Me. I desire your companionship and your fellowship, but you continue to allow the worldly things cloud your minds, your hearts, and your wills.

You cannot give Me your heart, your mind, and your will and hold some back for yourself. I desire to teach you the things to help you to survive the darkness, but I cannot do this without total submission to Me. You struggle daily in trying to figure out which way you want to go.

You do not have much time to figure this out My children. I have lost sheep out there that I need you to bring back into the herd, back into the grazing fence where they are protected. How can I give you these tools and teach you of these ways if you cannot place your feet on the solid foundation and not waver?

I want to save My lost children. I want the captives to be set free, the sick to be healed, and the lame to walk, and so many other miracles to perform. Today I need you to completely dedicate yourself to Me.

I need you to come before Me with a humble heart and give Me all control. As you do this you will find that things will become easier, the bad news won't be so bad, and you will be fully confident in faith that I am right there beside you. As you do this you will find out that your strength truly lies in Me and in My presence. I love you My children.

Submit yourself to Me, praise Me, put your complete faith in Me, and know that I your Heavenly Father will take care of you and will never leave you nor forsake you. Do what I have asked.

Take your steps in Me, and I will provide you with the tools of survival and the tools to carry out My work, My desires, and My miracles that I am asking you to do. Trust Me and let Me have all and complete control.

2 Peter 8:5-8
****

TILL YOUR GROUND IN YOUR HEARTS AND MIND

My children, today I want you to till your ground. Prepare your hearts and minds, so I can implant the words, wisdom, and the anointing that I have to give you. I want to pull up the old roots of the wild weeds that have been settled into your minds and your hearts.

I want to start with a fresh soil, ready to be seeded and fertilized with My knowledge and wisdom from My Heavenly realm. In order for this to happen you must set your mind and your hearts upon Me. You must give Me all parts of your minds and your hearts.

My children you all hold onto so much of your own understanding and desires that do not line up with My Word. It causes you to have multiple downfalls. Why will you not let Me do the rearranging I need to do to allow the supernatural to become natural for you?

You cannot understand the supernatural with the carnal minds that you hold onto. Allow Me to do the works, to plant a new harvest in your minds and your hearts. Let Me get rid of the old junk, the old doctorine, the old religion that you have allowed to close your minds to the things that I am trying to teach you in this end time hour.

Do not put Me in a box. Do not put limitations on Me. If you put limitations on Me then I cannot do the complete works or get you deep into the things that I have for you.

Begin to till your ground in your hearts and minds this day. Be at peace knowing that I am doing new things and great works inside each of My children as they surrender to the changes that I want to do. It will be these children who I truly will allow them to live in the supernatural above all the darkness of this world.

Praise Me and get into My Word. Open up all of your minds and hearts and allow the plowing and weeding to begin. There is not much time for this process to take place. You must do your part today.

Break down the limitations and the walls that you have allowed to be built around your minds and your hearts and know that I am doing a new thing with My children. Know that in this new thing that I am doing will become the transformation that you will need to survive in Me.

Apply the tools that I have been teaching you and get ready for the process to truly begin.

Mark 4: 13-20

****

LET GO OF THE WORLDLY THINGS

Let go of all the worldly cares. Let go of all the little worldly things. Put away the things of the cell phones, the movies, the internet, the books, etc. that are not focused on Me. Tune in to My praise. Tune in to My Word. Tune in to My knowledge. Focus upon Me.

Give Me this day. See how I move in your life. Rest in Me. Let Me flood you with My peace in all things; even the very small things… involve Me in there.

I am not saying I want you to put these things away. I am asking you to just involve Me. Praise Me, study on My Word, watch movies to feed your spirit on things of Me, read on the news that I have for you in My Word... Make Me a focal point of the day. Rest in Me.

Let Me flood you with My peace in all things, even the very small things… involving Me in there. Focus upon My Word of truth that I will give unto you this day. Allow Me to have you in My presence. Sup at My table.

Do I not ask you to be an example unto My little children? How do they know if it is always hidden and done in quiet? They need to see by example how to involve Me into your life, into your day. Let Me be the center of your day and just see what I do for you.

Be joyful in Me. Have gladness and laughter in your voice. If you cannot rejoice in Me in all things, in all seasons, how are you expecting to have it in the darkness?

I want to spend time with you today My children. Come and spend time with Me. Enjoy your time with Me today. Become an example to all of those around you of what it really means to have dined and to be focused on Me, your Father.

Come into My presence and fellowship with Me. You will experience a new anointing today as you do these things. Let Me share this time with you. Allow Me to give you this experience with

Me. Sit with Me in the heavenly place and know that you have truly been with your Father today. I love you My children, and I am just waiting on you.

Psalm 118:24

****

START YOUR DAY WITH JOY AND LAUGHTER

My children, My heart rejoices in your efforts that you have tried to spend time with Me. I want you to get into the habit of taking Me and including Me, evolving Me into your daily activities.

Take Me in your car when you drive. Take Me on a walk. Take Me to dinner with you. Spend time with Me as you would the love of your life, your best friend, you favorite person. I want to hear all the desires of your heart. I want to be the one who you take with you were ever you go.

I want to be able to show you at any time one of My lost sheep that I need you to bring to My feet. But how can you do this if you are not carrying Me with you at all time? How can you tell them about sitting at My feet if you have not done it yourself?

There are many things I desire from My children, but today. I desire to hear the sweet voices of happiness of My children. I want joy to overflow, bubbling out like a pot that is overflowing from hot water. I want that joy to be spread out to all those around you.

How do you think that the hurt and dying are looking for? They are not looking for what they already have. They do not want to see people who are complaining, hurting one another, sad, angry, and not living what it is that My children claim that life with Me really is. They already have misery. They want the fire, the love, the compassion, the joy, and they want the opposite of what they have now.

I want you to practice having joy. I want you to smile when you feel like you can't. It is in this time that you will find the breakthrough. Joy is what gives you strength in Me.

Joy is what helps My light shine through you. It is the magnet that will draw in My lost sheep. And with joy you will not focus on all the circumstances. You will focus on Me and allow Me to take care of the circumstances instead of trying to take them in your own hands and make them a bigger mess.

Start your day today with joy and laughter. Take a few moments of your time today and sit and talk to Me. Allow the joy to just bubble up inside. Talk about the good that is in your life.

Let this joy overtake your atmosphere and spread it to all around you. Let them see that I am a God that wants My children happy and joyful. Sing praises to Me from your joy.

Watch the angry people around you have their anger just melt as you stay joyful around them. Do not let them bring you to their level My children. You must stay at your level.

This is one of the keys of survival in the days ahead. You must stay joyful and in the higher heavenly realm with Me and not allow the devastation and sins of this world bring you down to them. And to stay there will be through the strength of your joy and the only way to strengthen your joy is to practice it.

Today find your joy. Strengthen your joy. For I truly do desire to share this joy with you as we continue to spend time together in all you do. Share it with all you know and rest assured that I am right here to help you keep your joy. All you have to do is ask.

Nehemiah 8:10
****

TAKE THIS JOURNEY WITH ME

My children, I want you today to take a journey with Me. I want you to look at all that I have prepared you with. I have given you everything that you need to take this journey with Me. I need you to take My hand today.

Give Me every emotion of unhappiness, unworthiness, sadness, anger, bitterness, unforgiveness and let Me replace it with these things that I have been teaching you.

I need you to let Me replace them with humbleness, peace, joy, happiness, songs of praises in your heart, your mind on Me, to be in My presence. Let Me give you these as you come on this journey with Me because how can you love without them? I need you to learn these things to be able to walk in My total agape love.

There is much darkness and evil things that are here and more that is getting ready to happen. There is much devastation coming to this land. I want to protect you the same as I did for Abraham, but you must learn these things that I am teaching you to survive. There is so little time. I cannot express this enough My children.

The only way to be protected is to know My survival tools to actively practice these tools. How do you learn to properly use a hammer if you do not practice using it? How do you become an electrician if you do not understand the laws and tools and how electric works if you do not study it and practice what you learn?

The same is what I am trying to teach you My children that you cannot do these things just one day. They must continuously stay active in your daily lives.

Come away with Me on this journey. Give Me time in your day today and just sit in My presence and allow Me to do the works that needs to be done so you can continue to practice these tools that I am giving you.

Let Me reprogram your Mind. Let Me reformat the way you think. Allow Me to rebuild that which is destroyed and replace it with My thoughts, My understanding, and My knowledge. Allow Me to give you the mind like My Son.

Come away with Me and let Me inject My agape love that I so desire to give to you. I do not want My children to parish. I only desire for My children to have the very best.

I want you to be complete equip for the journeys I want to take you on, for the war in the natural and spiritual that you are going to face, and to equip you to be under My wings to be able to do for you what the world will not be able to do.

They will see that I, your God am real. They will not be able to stand before Me and say that they do not know there is a God because all will know. Do not be too late and get caught in the devastation that is going to happen.

As you come into this journey with Me, you will feel My presence, and you will know that I have done the works that you are in need of. You will know that I have done the rearranging and rebuilding to allow the steps to survival in Me to take place.

Do not let this day go by without coming into My presence and allow Me to take you, hand in hand, into the changing journey of your life. Allow Me to get you in that place with Me that all the things of this world will not touch you.

As you come into this journey with Me, you will have all that I have equipped you with and so much more. You will be able to continue to pick up the tools ahead and use them as I completely reveal them to you.

You cannot do this with your mind on the world. You must have your mind focus upon Me. Communicate with Me, and I will give you all that you are in need of.

Many of you, My children, I have given you instructions, after instructions, step by step, but you have not yet done those things that I have given you to do. Go back to those words that I have given you. Regroup and list these things that you have not done and do them. As you do this, all the rest will become easier and a new understanding will take place.

Put your mind on Me, sit in My presence, and let Me take you into the secret place of the Most High. Give Me your mind, your body, your spirit, your soul, and your will. Allow Me to implant these things in you that will strengthen you in the days ahead.

I love you, My children. I desire for you come away with Me. Come away with Me and take this journey with Me. Do not waste time. Do not procrastinate. Do not tell Me, you have no time and you are too busy. Do not let time run out. Just reach out and take My hand.

Submit to Me and let Me do the necessary things that need to be done for you to be able to carry My agape love which in turn will equip you completely with all the tools I have given you so far to beat the darkness and devastation.

The journey is here for you to take. So take that first step and take My hand and let's go. Then I will do the rest. I will be waiting for you today with My hand stretch out, just waiting for you to grab it.

Matthew 11:28-30; Jeremiah 29:11; Isaiah 55:6-9
****

NEED TO INTERCEDE

My children, many of you are not taking Me seriously. The handful of those who are taking Me serious will need to understand that I do not want what is coming.

My heart aches for what is about to happen. I need you today to intercede for those who are falling behind. I need My children today to check themselves and then stand up and really intercede for the rest of My children to wake up before it is too late. They must understand that if they do not straighten up they will be closed to Me and My church forever.

Please understand My little ones who are faithful that as these devastations occur, you must continue to stay on My path. You must continue to use the tools that I am and will give you.

You cannot allow sorrow, sadness, bitterness, anger, resentment, or the sense of loss have any part in you. Don't start questioning Me as these things happen. You have to leave it in My hands and praise Me through the storm of destruction and correction.

The ones who fall into this destruction and devastation has done so because they would not pay the price. They would not take Me serious. They would not follow My instructions or guidance. They would not leave My truly anointed alone and get themselves right with me. They would not allow Me to be the focus of their lives and truly follow me. I have to fulfill My sentencing that I will have past as judgment.

Intercede, little ones, pray like you have never prayed before. You must understand you are about to witness many love ones fall away.

You are about to witness many loved ones be destroyed by the hand of the enemy. This is because they will have made their choice for the last time. They will not be able to enter My sanctuary or My place that I have to help those who truly have not had the chance.

And some who will try will be put to death. Some it will be spiritually and others will be naturally.

I have given My instructions. I have given My warnings to heed. But they still continue to ignore Me. They continue to think that they still have time. They have no time.

My children, desperately seek My face. Get as close to Me as you can. Please do not become disheartened as these things take place because it is something that has to take place for the ones who have not known Me to get the chance.

I have called many times to the ones who are getting ready to go through this horrible time. If they would only listen, if they would have only done the things that I have ask them to do. But they chose not to do these things.

Although this is happening to them, you must praise Me and be joyful through it all because you cannot allow the destruction and darkness take you over. And it will if you do not use these tools that I am trying to teach you.

But for today, My children, seek My face. Pray and intercede for those to wake up quickly and also for those who will have to be a witness and affective by it that they will continue to be strong.

Pray from your heart. Pray for those who you love. Do not give up until I tell you to give up. I do not wish for these events to take place, but I will do what I have to do.

I need My church to be HOLY, and you must understand I will have a HOLY church no matter what the cost. But I promise you as you pray today, a peace that passes all understanding will come over you.

I will keep you. I will not leave you nor forsake you. You will still be able to praise Me and have the joy in your heart that you are going to need to get through this very dark time and hour.

But you must keep your eyes on Me at all times. Do not sway from My path because even though this devastation and destruction is coming, much rejoicing will be coming as well. Many blessings are coming and will be received, but first, I must perfect My church.

Do what I ask of you today My children and know that all will be well.

Numbers 3:5-10

****

REPENT AND MAKE A COVENANT

My children, to those who are faithful and are seeking Me I am well pleased. It is ever so important to stay on My path right now. Stay in My presence like never before. The devastation is beginning and so is My judgment on the church.

There are many out there leading My lost children further away from Me. There is sin so ramped around you, and it is truly destroying this Earth on its own. But it is time to cause devastations and circumstance to get the attention of those who I desire to come to My feet and destroy those who will not serve Me after knowing Me.

There is only a small window being opened for the back sliders; after this window is closed it will be remain that way. The all-consuming fire is coming. I am calling all My children to repentance. Those who truly repent and sell out to Me 100% will not be affected by the devastations or circumstances, because I the Lord your God will protect you.

My children, today, I want you to come with Me in true repentance and determine, with no turning back, to serve Me with everything in you. After you repent and make this covenant with Me, rejoice for you will have step into My glory realm.

You will know what it is like to truly be protected by the most high God. Rejoice in Me that you have listen to My heeding and you will know that you will be safe through all that is going to happen.

Do not be sadden because of the lost souls, they had their chance, but rejoice for all the souls that will be saved and will be given the chance to know Me.

Today, complete turn away from your sin nature, repent, and rejoice in Me. I will make known to My true children who is of Me and who is not.

It is also redemption time. I will uplift those who are truly serving me. Also, I will give you step by step directions as I did for all My children in the past of exactly what to do and when to move. I am raising you up in this hour to 100% serve Me and to bring in My harvest.

Even though this devastation is coming, so is the blessings. Do not let the devastation worry you or cause you to doubt and waiver from Me. Just put your trust in Me that all is well with My children and this judgment will not harm you, My good and faithful servants.

If I can make away for Joshua and Jerusalem to cross the Jordan, If I can warn my prophet Jeremiah what is about to happen, If I can warn My prophet Isaiah of what is going to happen to the wicked then why would I not do the same for you.

For those of you who are in lust and want to cause deception and pride in My churches, I will strip you of all your fancies, of all your wealth, and glamour and will make known who you truly are. I am giving you a small opportunity to repent this day. To turn from your evil ways and your sin nature that is causing you to fall away from Me and join the ones who l will protect in this given time.

Now My children when I say lust I am not just speaking of the sexual lust. I am also speaking of the lust for this world, the desires of what others have been given, the lust for power. Do not be so quick to judge. If you judge My anointed children ones who have truly repented then you will fall under the punishment that is coming.

Do not fall into these traps. My heart desires of you this day for you to truly repent, make this commitment to Me, and rejoice in My presence. Give Me true praises from your heart and watch My miracles take place during this time of punishment and correction.

I am a loving God, but I am also one that seeks justice for My children. Do what I have asked and let Me have all control. Be encouraged this day and choose to serve Me, your Heavenly Father.

My hand is outstretched all you have to do is grab it and hold on tight, and I will do the rest. Saith the Lord your God.

Jeremiah 3:11-25; Isaiah 3
****

GIVE ME YOUR TONGUE

Listen to Me well today, My children. Keep an eye on your tongue. Many are falling short because they cannot fight the temptation to put another down. Whether it is right or wrong in what you say, I have called you to be a people who are kind, understanding, and to carry out My will and have My heart. Does My Word not say, "He who is without sin cast the first stone?"

There is no person on the Earth who is without sin. Only one man walked Earth without sin, and He chose to give up His life for you. He is always sitting at My right hand ever interceding for you. Everyone has done Him wrong, taken what He has done for granted, rejected Him, caused Him much misery, and much pain. Yet He still stands in the gap for you, so you can have your chance to be here with Me in Glory.

What makes you think you have the right to come against any of My children? Who are you to say they are not doing what I have called them to do if I have not revealed it to you?

There are many things that I have called My children to do and there are steps that they will have to take to get there. But it does not mean that it is not in My plan just because you do not agree with it.

If you truly want to know about something, it is Me you should be asking. If I want you to know, then I will reveal it to you. If I do not reveal it to you then leave it in My hands. Do not go spouting off of the mouth for it is then that you cause curses and trouble upon yourself.

Yes there are some children who have hardened their hearts to Me one too many times. I have asked you to shake the dust off your feet to them, and to keep moving forward and not turn back. This does not give you the right to talk about these children because it causes Me to have My hands tied in vindicating you. Let it go. Let Me take care of it.

Yes, I need you to warn those it may hurt. Let those express their hurt to heal. However, do not let it become idle talk.

The devil is coming full force to attack My children through their minds and their tongues. You must use all that I have taught you thus far, to keep these things clean. Yes, I know there are times when things need to be discussed, but it should never be for putting down, but to find a way to uplift through prayer or encouragement.

Yes, I know there are times that I have you gather in times where plans and strategies need to be communicated and things need to be dealt with. But judgment should never be a part of this. Those who have caused My anointed to suffer greatly, they will be receiving their punishment, but do not take pleasure in their punishment.

Give Me your tongues this day. Know that if you do this I will keep you from causing your own spiritual death. I will do all that I promised. I will protect, guide, instruct, and lead the way. But you first must give Me all control and that also includes your mouth and your thoughts.

Today let your tongues become a tool of praise and to be used for My kingdom and not of destruction on My children. Let your tongues be a tool to tear down the enemy's kingdom not build it up. Do not allow the enemy to use your tongue to open any doors for him to come and cause you destruction in your lives.

Focus today on changing the way you speak and watch the difference it makes. Let My Spirit lead you, and you will know if what you are saying is ok or not. If it is not ok, quickly repent, and do not do it again.

Yes things must be communicated to solve problems or to know how to intercede. Do not allow false condemnation to stop you from continuing to teach My children how to intercede. Ask for My discernment on what I am expecting out of you.

Today ask Me to cleanse your tongue. Dedicate your tongue to Me. Allow Me to control your tongue and watch the miracles begin. As you allow this to happen, you are allowing My Holy Spirit to speak for you and many souls will be watching in amazement on just how much changing the tongue will effect what they think.

I cannot bless a defiled tongue. So give Me your tongue this day. Let Me do the cleansing. Sing praise with this tongue to Me. And watch the breakthroughs come.

Destroy the enemy's kingdom and camp through the power of your tongue as you speak the Words that My Son has given you in My Word. He left you with the authority by using His name to tear the enemy apart, now use the tool of the tongue to do so.

You have committed to follow Me with all your heart, but today I am requiring your tongue.

James 3:3-9; Matthew 10:14; John 8:7
****

SPEND TIME WITH ME

Oh My children! Today I want to spend time with you. I want to go for a walk with you, take a drive with you, or just sit in a quiet spot with you. I want you to take a small spot in your day just to visit with Me. I know of all the needs and desires. But today, I just want you to find peace in My presence and just talk to Me.

It does not have to be anything big. I just long to communicate with you and just take a few moments and enjoy each other. I want to just spend time with My children.

I want some alone time with you. I want to tell you secrets and words of love into your beings. That is all I want from you today is a small part of your time.

I want you to just take a moment and let the things of this world go into the background and take a small journey with Me. Take a break from this world and come into the Heavenly realm and find peace, My children. Find your peace in Me.

I am waiting for you to come and spend time with Me. I love you, My children. Oh, how I love you. Please come and talk with Me and find the peace and rest that you need.

Isaiah 30:18; Proverbs 8:17; Philippians 4:4-7
****

LOVE YOURSELF TO LOVE OTHERS

Today is a day of love, righteousness, and faith. Today is a day that you should be coming into My house to praise Me with all of your hearts, no matter what is going on around you. No matter how much sleep you got, or what has happen to you this week. If you are worried about these things your eyes are not upon Me.

How can you come into My house and not pour out your love on those in My house? Is it not My commandment "to love thy neighbor as thyself"? What saddens My heart is most of you do not love yourself, so then I ask how can you love your neighbor? When you do not love yourself how can you love Me for I have created you? These are questions I ask of you this day.

If you see your brother or sister in need and you turn away from them, yet you tell Me that you would do anything for Me, where is the truth in your words or actions? You say but Lord what do I have to give? It is by faith that you should give knowing that if it is of Me I will return it back to you.

If you speak wrongly against your brother or sister, how is that showing love? I have called you to be My children of love, so how can I really bless you if you cannot show love to others as I have shown love to you?

To love yourself you must be content on who you are. You must accept that I have made you the way you are but also be willing to let Me change you to conform you to the ways that I need you to do the works in My kingdom.

Allow Me to take away the things of this world that conform you to be things that you are not. Do you not know that as you put yourself down, you also put Me down?

When you speak words of discontentment into the air about yourself you open the door to allow the enemy to have an area to fight you in? You also cause curses upon yourself. Now I am not saying to be obsessed with yourselves. I am not saying to be prideful or arrogant. I am saying that you need to just love the fact that you are you.

Allow Me to love you through you. You must love yourself enough to take care of yourself spiritually and naturally. You need to see your worth as I see it. If you are bound up with thoughts of unworthiness, dirtiness, or unusableness then how can I use you to bring in My lost souls to Me and love them through you?

You are to have My heart are you not? And My children, I truly do love you. If you cannot love yourself ask Me to let you see yourself through My eyes.

As you learn to do this, then you can truly love Me. You will then be open to know that I can love you, that you are someone worth loving because you will not hold onto the limitations that you cannot be loved.

As you truly love Me, you will then allow Me to fully use you to love through you. If you have yielded in this area then how then would it not be easy to love your brother or sister because then you would be doing it through Me.

As you strive for this perfection of loving, you will also be striving for righteousness. You cannot be righteous without love and you cannot love anyone unless you start with yourself. To love yourself, you have to have faith in Me to know that I have made you the way you are and that I will use you because I made you and I desire to.

So today, allow Me to show you how I see you and how you are worthy to be loved and you will learn what true love for Me really is and it will change your life.

Today find your love for yourself, your brother and your sister, and your true love for Me. Step out in faith today and say, "I love myself as God loves me, and I open myself to truly love God, and I will also love my brother and sister as my God would love them. I will strive to be a walker of love and strive to be a righteous person whom my

God can work through and love those around me the way He would".

Today ponder on the questions I have asked of you. Begin this true journey of love and see how much you will no longer see the bad inside of yourself, but the good.

Then you can truly open yourself to truly be used by Me with no limitations of self-worth. See how I will truly love through you to other people around you, and you will see the lost souls be drawn in with the love that will surround you.

James 2:8; Mark 12:30-31

****

TAKING OUT THE TRASH

Today is taking out the trash day, My little ones. I want you today to admit to the garbage that is in your life. I want you to pick it up and throw it away. You do this by coming to Me with true repentance.

You need to ask Me to truly forgive you for all the junk that you have let accumulate in your life. It is time to lighten the load and admit to your wrong doings. I cannot bless a mess.

As you come to Me in true repentance and tell Me of all these things that you have left laying around in your life, I will throw them into the sea of forgetfulness, where they are remember no more. I will dispose of the trash.

Allow Me to lighten these burdens off your shoulders and get rid of the dirt that keeps your soul from being clean. I need your temples clean to do My works and to be able to use you to perform My great and marvelous miracles. I need the mess to be gone so that the blessings can truly start to roll in. Time is so very short, My little ones.

It is time to get rid of all this extra weight My children. In the very near future you will have to be carrying very lightly. You will not be able to survive with all this trash that you are letting yourself be burden down with. The darkness that is here will be growing much worse. You cannot allow the garbage - sin in your life slow you down.

It is time to clean up today, My children. Search your hearts, your minds, your thoughts, your life, and your soul. Come to Me with the truth of what you know is in there cluttering up your walk with Me. Allow Me to do assist you with the cleaning. It is time to get rid of all those things that of the world that you do not need.

Then I want you to renew yourself with the things that are good, true and pure. Renew yourself in Me. Renew yourself in My Word, in My presence, and in My praise. I want you to put into practice the things that I have been teaching you. I want you to count all the good things that I have been doing in your life.

As you get rid of all this negative things in your life today, reinforce it with the positive. Praise Me. Give Me thanks for all that is going right in your life, and for the things that I have promised you and will come to pass.

Learn to praise Me no matter what you are going through. Learn to be happy no matter what the circumstances show you. For it is in Me that you get your strength.

It is Me that you will get your peace. And it is through My Son's blood and My forgiveness that you will become clean this day.

Micah 7:18-19; Philippians 4:7-13
****

TRUST THAT I PROVIDE FOR YOU

My beloved and stubborn children, I have looked upon you this day and I have seen a lack of trust in Me. As a child, did you not look at the ones who were responsible for you to take care of you? You would do this without hesitation. You would do this expecting your needs to be met.

I am the creator of all things, yet you, My children, fail to trust Me. You ask Me of many things, but you want Me to do them on your terms, on your timing, and according to the way you want them to happen. You give Me stipulations on your blessings and miracles. I am not a God that tolerates limitations. I expect to be given the trust of 100% to do the things that My children have asked according to My plan for their lives.

I have promised to provide and protect My children, but you fail to allow Me to do these things. You allow your natural eyes to take back what you have asked. You have said to Me by doing this, "Lord, I do not believe that you are capable." I am telling you this day, take your eyes off the natural. Quit questioning the things that I am doing. I am working on your behalves.

I am providing for My children as they completely trust Me. Some blessings cannot come until I have set certain foundations. Some blessings cannot come until you untie My hands. Some blessings cannot come until I have finished what I have set out to accomplish while you are placed in the circumstances that you are in.

Do not think of it as a foolish thing of the things that I have given you or the places that I have you at. Do not assume that the reason you are in your circumstance has anything to do with you. I have some of you placed where you are so that I can do the works in others that need to be done by having you where you are at.

Have you not said, "Whatever it takes Lord; whatever the cost Lord, I will do; use me Lord"? You have told Me these things through your mouths and your hearts. As you put your trust truly in Me

100% you will be able to rise above your circumstance. You will be able to see that even when you do not understand the things that I have done, you will know that I am in control. You will see that I will provide all of your needs. You need not to depend on man for anything. I am your father and I will provide. Learn this now My little ones. This is a major key on how to survive in these end times.

Today, I need you to set your minds on the Victory! I need you to set in your minds that I will be there at all times. I will deliver you. I will not allow you to go under. Set your mind on trusting Me 100%.

Praise Me this day with all of your heart that I am all that you truly need to do anything in this life. I want you to praise Me for all that I have, am, and will be doing in your life. Praise Me that I am strengthening your trust in Me. Praise Me for all the Victories that you will have from this day forth.

Quit questioning what I am doing and trust that I am working everything out for your good and My glory. I did mighty things for My children before, why would I be any different now? I have saved My children from floods, famines, kings, themselves, murderers, armies, ….and the list goes on.

Today get in your mind that I will do all this for you and even greater things as you continue to follow Me and truly trust Me 100%, praise Me, and put all your faith in Me knowing that I your God and Father will always come through for you. I am that I am. I will do all things that I have said I will do as you give Me full control and allow Me to straighten the path to get you to the place to receive all that I have for you.

Praise Me this day, that My love will forever be yours, and My Word is your protection, and I am your strength. I am your Father and your provider. Praise Me this day that all of these things are being done for you.

Psalm 118
****

43

PRAISE FOR VICTORY

Praise Me! Praise Me! For everything in your life, praise Me. It is redemption time. It is time to look at the score board and realize that through Me you have won the Victory. My Angels sit in the bleachers cheering you on, letting you know that the victory is yours.

It is time to tell My lost sheep how I have turned your life around on the scoreboard. It is time to hold your head up high and tackle all the things that come your way with confidence that the game is already won.

It is time to know that it is the season of setting the records straight. It is time to allow the scoreboards to speak for themselves. It is time for those who have cursed you and put you down to see it was I, the Lord your God, who was in complete control. It is time that My glory is seen throughout the land. Today, celebrate in Me that you have won the victory, and the blessings are here and the souls are coming in.

Now yes, there will be times when the enemy will try to tackle you down again. But you need to keep your eyes upon Me and know that the Victory is yours. Even when it looks like something has happened and you have been defeated, know that as I protected Paul when he was stoned and made it look like he was dead, that I will do the same thing for you. I will protect you through all the evil of this world.

All you have to do is be determined to continue to follow Me, show the world that they may have thought they stoned you to death, but it was I that protected you and it is I that has allowed you to continue to serve Me and do My works, greater than before. It is I that has resurrected you because I have called you and would not allow man to destroy you.

Praise Me! Praise Me! Praise Me! I want you to know with everything in you that I will bring My rain from the heavens, I will produce the fruit to be good fruit, I will prosper you in all that you

44

do. I will keep you in all the seasons of your life. Spread My good news and know that you have the victory.

Praise Me this day, My little ones that you will continue to do My works and that your prosperity is here. It is time to bring in the harvest. It is time to for you to praise Me for the breakthrough. It is here. You have won this Victory.

So Praise Me with every part of your being! Praise Me, and as you praise Me, you will know that I am doing all that I said I would do. Tackle all these things in your life with praise for you have won the Victory. Now claim it this day and PRAISE ME!

Acts 14:15-20

****

PRINCE AND PRINCESS OF THE MOST HIGH

My children, how can you do My work if your head is in the hole, you refuse to get up out of your valleys, or keep your eyes on the circumstances instead of on Me? I have a plan and a purpose in your life that I would love for you to fulfill.

I have a plan to keep you protected, fed, and able to go out and spread My Words, My love, and My salvation that I give through My son to people throughout the nations. But your mindset is still not where it needs to be. You hang your head low. You hide in the corners. You do not expect Me to do what you have asked Me to do. You decide that either you do not deserve it or only you can provide it.

So I ask you today, are you not King's kids? Does a prince or princess hold their heads down? No. A prince and princess hold their heads up high. They know that they are well taken care of. But they too have a work to do. They too have responsibilities, duties, and serve the ones that they are over. Many problems with the prince and princess are the mindsets that they get caught up in themselves.

But a true prince and princess of the Almighty King will know where they stand with Me. They will hold their head up high. They will know that I, their Father has their best interest in the plan and will do all that I have said I would do. They will defend their honor and the honor of their Father, the kingdom, and for the people. They battle with the people of all kinds to defend their kingdom. They protect their inheritance and claim what is rightfully theirs. Why do you think you are any different?

I am calling you to have a mindset of a prince and princess of the Most High God. And also I am calling you to know that you are a servant as well. You are My servants. You must find the balance of the two, so that you can begin to walk in all My fullness and blessing that I have for you. Boldness, confidence, and faith are what you need in this hour to receive that in which I have for you.

Do not think of this as a strange thing that I am asking of you. You say, "Lord, I have asked and not received". So I say to you this day, claim it like royality and know that in the appointed time it will be done.

But also remember you must do all that I have ask of you as well. I do not need spoiled, selfish, and ungrateful children. I do require that you take the steps that I have ask you to take, to learn of the royal hood, to learn of the servant hood and then I will take the final steps and then all will be in place.

So today I am instructing you to look into My Word and see all that you shall inherit and claim it. Look into My Word and see what I expect out of My servants. Then make up your mind that you will do these things that I require of you.

Put on the mind of Christ, the royal prince of the Almighty King, and know it will also be the mind of royal hood and servant hood. For My Son is a true prince and a servant and that is exactly what I have called you to be. My Son is and always will be the example that you must follow. Lift your head up high this day, find your inheritance in Me, find the steps you have to do, and claim it.

Jeremiah 29:11; John 1:12
****

CELEBRATE

Celebrate My children. It is time for the festivals to begin. The war is not over, but My people of old did not stop celebrating because the war was still going on.

They would use the praise they gave Me and the celebrations that they would have to restore their strength and renew their spirit to fight. They would celebrate to still be alive. They would celebrate the soon return of their soldiers. They would celebrate the chance to soon be able to be sent out in the battle themselves. They would welcome the idea of Victory.

Yes, you must still fight. You must still continue to battle in the war. But do not stop celebrating.

Praise Me that I have strengthened you. Thank Me that you will have this day to be joyous in Me. Praise Me that all is well. The enemy will not win. You will have a mind of Victory. As you have a mind of Victory, praise on your heart, and the sword in your hand, you will know that victory is upon you.

Put on your armor today. But be ready for celebrating at the evening for another battle will be won. The breakthroughs are going to start coming in and blessing upon blessings are pouring in. You cannot win the war with just a battle ready mind. It will make you weak and weary. You must stay strong in praise. For it is in praise that the battle is truly won.

Celebrate My children Celebrate in Me. Celebrate in all My promises. Celebrate in your inheritance. Celebrate of the chance to serve Me. Celebrate in Me in the darkness for it will bring you light.

As My servant Moses and My people praised Me and Celebrate their victory over pharaoh even before the victory was finished, so should you do the same. They praised and celebrated their victory through Me and then as soon as the victory was over the women followed. They gave Me all the honor and glory. I was there with them the whole time given instructions and showing them the way to go. This battle was won and celebration took place. As you follow this example others around you will see and know that it is through praise and celebration that the victory comes.

You must know, I will never leave you nor forsake you. The enemy would love for you to believe that I would, but I have promised you over and over in My Word that I will never leave you. I will be right by your side at all times through the battle, in the quiet times, through the celebrations, and in all times. I have proven it over and over.

If the enemy tries to use this against you, you tell him, "get behind me satan for it is written, use Deuteronomy 31:8 (NIV) and personalize saying, *The* LORD *himself goes before me and will be with me; He will never leave me nor forsake me. I will not be afraid; I will not be discouraged."* Tell satan to take his lies far from you in the name of My Son, Jesus and he must flee and leave you alone.

Why do you think it is so hard for you to be happy? The enemy wants you to be defeated and saddened. He knows that if you are happy and celebrating in Me that your strength will become greater. He knows that he will no longer be able to get you to focus on the circumstances and that you will be totally focused on Me.

He will know that anything he sends your way will not have any effect on you because you will have learned to be happy in Me, praise Me, and celebrate in My name that the battles will be won and then the war. He knows that as you are focused on Me and as you serve Me and as you start claiming your inheritance, he is losing ground and more battles are going to be won against him.

Fight in Me today, Serve for Me today, Thank Me in advance that the battles are being won, and in the evening celebrate in Me that the battles has been won no matter what the eye sees, breakthroughs are coming, blessings are flowing, and your inheritance is being restored.

Celebrate with one another or just with Me, but celebrate that I will keep you through all of this and is right by your side. Keep your head up high. And celebrate in Me! Strengthen your spirit on Me for I cannot use a weary solider to fight the front line or in this darkness! Celebrate and praise in Me and the strength will be there to renew you!

Read Exodus 15 for the praises of Moses and the Israelites to God and then of Mariam and the women followed.

Psalm 149:6; 2 Chronicles 20:17-22

****

SUBMIT TO MY PLAN AND PURPOSE FOR YOU

Put everything into My hands and give Me all control. I am the same God today, as I was yesterday, and I will remain the same God forever. I have a plan and purpose for your life, but you have to give Me full control.

Today, hand Me everything in, around, and through your life. Give Me full control to do the
changes, rearranging, building, separating, and destroying that I need to do. The only thing I am asking from you is to just surrender it all to Me and give Me control.

Ask Me to cleanse you the way that David had asked Me to cleanse him, and I will do so with the blood of My Son. Turn your life over to My control and allow Me to do all the works that I need to do to make you the vessels that I need in this hour.

Completely submit to Me and My plan for your life. Let Me set you on the path to your destiny. This is all I am asking of you today.

Psalms 102:25-27; Malachi 3:6; Hebrews 13:8;
Ephesians 1:11; Psalm 51
****

RENEWAL AND THE HOLY SPIRIT

I want to renew your anointing this day. I want to strengthen the mantle that lay upon you, My children. My children, you are growing weary because you still do not keep your eyes totally focused upon Me.

You allow yourself to get overwhelmed, and you do not stay under My peace that I have given you access to. Yes, I know of your hardships, but I have provide you a comforter, My Holy Spirit.

I desire to renew you this day as you come into My house to worship and praise Me. I want to strengthen you as you come into My house to be fed My Word. I want you to be determined to no longer look at your circumstances but to look at Me. Give Me your burdens.

If I have not told you or asked you to do them, and you are overwhelmed then let it go. I cannot
use a weary soldier or servant to do My work. I need you strong in Me. As you do turn your eyes upon Me, your anointing will grow even stronger in Me.

I want you to everyday invite Me into your day. I want you to cover yourself in My Son's blood every day. I want you to be consumed with the Holy Spirit every day. I want you this day to make a commitment to walk in the Holy Spirit.

You must walk in the Holy Spirit at all times to be able to do My work that I have called you to do. I need you to do this so that I can show you what a person truly has in the heart so you will know how to minister in Me or just walk away.

I want to show you those who are demon possessed and how to set them free. I want you to hear My voice for yourself and be able to follow instructions just like I did for My Son, Jesus and My servant, Paul and many other ones that truly served Me. Signs, miracles and wonders followed them because they were led by My Holy Spirit.

My Son was so filled with the Holy Spirit that just a touch of His garment could be used to perform miracles. My servant Paul was so anointed that he would take cloths and anoint them and then people would take them to the sick to be healed. It was because they walked in the Holy Spirit that they could do these things. I want you My children to want to walk in this same anointing.

I want you to desire to do these things in Me. I need you to be willing vessels to do this to bring in the lost and dying souls to My kingdom. Will you commit to walk in the Holy Spirit everyday this day? Will you allow Me to renew your anointing in Me? Will you allow Me to strengthen your mantle that I have given you? Or will I have to pass your mantle on to another willing vessel?

I love you My children. I desire you to bring in My harvest. I desire to have My signs, miracles, and wonders to start flowing. I need you to allow Me to do this for you and for you to make this commitment to Me this day so I can use you in this hour, My children.

Acts 10:38; Acts 13:2; Acts 13:9-10; Acts 15:8;
Acts 16:6-7; Acts 19:11-12
****

COMFORT IN ME

I want you to find comfort in Me this day. I want you to allow Me to place a peace, love, and a security in your hearts and in your souls, that I the Lord God, will take care of you. You are My children. I am your Father. I delight in My children's happiness.

I want you to seek My presence today. I want you to close your eyes for a moment today, and go for a walk with Me. Take a journey with Me. I want you today to experience the peace that you will find in My presence.

I want you to see yourself with Me hand in hand. I want you to know that I am right here by your side at all times. Find a quiet spot with Me today, I don't care where. Find a spot where it will be just you and Me.

I want to renew your hope in Me that I am in control of all things, and I only do things that is for your good. I did not say you would understand what I do, how I do it, and at times why. I do however want you to get back into that comfortable place of placing yourselves in My hands and knowing that I do not rest.

My eyes are always upon you. I hear your cries, your concerns, your heart's desire, your fears, your joys, and every prayer that you send to Me that reaches My throne room.

I want you to rest assure this day that I am right here with you through every part of your life. I am right here by your side to hold your hands, wipe your tears, and love you unconditionally.

As I am doing this for you this day, I want you to remember the love and peace that you will feel and spread it to everyone who comes across your path. I want you to allow Me to deposit My love inside of you to help renew and restore the ones around you through Me.

Give Me your troubles. Let Me have control over everything in your life. Let Me take this worry away from you and take the burdens from your shoulders that you are not meant to carry. Be strengthened in Me. Find your refreshment in Me.

Come away with Me today and rest in My arms. Allow Me to comfort you and renew these things in you this day. Come and take another journey with Me and be refreshed in My love. And remember as you experience this day, take it and spread it to everyone you meet.

Psalm 121; 1 John 4:7-12; John 14:27; Philippians 4:6-7
****

MAKE A DECISION

I am going to speak to the ones who have been heeding My voice. I can no longer wait for others to decide to leave the earthly things and follow Me totally with everything in them. I cannot wait for them to decide to pay the price that some of My children have paid and sat by waiting for others to get where they are.

So when I speak it today, it will be for you that have heeded to My voice and My calling. It will be for those who truly have decided to follow Me no matter what the cost.

I can no longer allow you, My children who are hungry and thirsty for Me to be sitting idly by. I want to open My heavens and pour out the miracle saving power, the stronger anointing, the supernatural things, and the blessings that I desire to give to My faithful ones.

My other children will have to decide to catch up or be left behind. They will either buckle down and decide to die out to their flesh and completely follow Me or they are going to miss the boat of the things that I am about to do.

You are going to see My anointing flow like you never have before. You are going be a witness to things untold of. You are going to see My glory stronger than you could ever imagine. Do not get discouraged now. Do not slack off or get leery of what I am doing.

Today, I want you to search your heart and get into that secret place with Me and know whether or not you are one of My children who has made this decision. If you are not sure, today is the day to get yourself right with Me completely. Seek My face today.

Pray for your brothers and sisters that they open their eyes to the truth. Pray that they decide to get aboard the boat and not to miss out on this move that I am bringing your way. This may very well be your last chance to be a part of this mighty move.

I am calling those who have truly sold out to Me. Are you one of those? Are you going to be a part of this mighty move that I am going to bring in the very near future? Will you be one of the ones who will miss the move because the flesh and worldly things were just too hard to give up for Me?

These questions I want you to ask yourselves this day. Find your answers and know where you stand with Me. Then pray to bring others to your level in Me.

My harvest is just waiting to be picked and brought into My house. I am ready to move. Prepare yourself this day. Do not miss out on what I am about to do.

Colossians 2:6-7; Hebrews 2:1-4
****

REJOICE IN ME AND AGAIN I SAY REJOICE!

Oh My faithful children, rejoice in Me always and again I say Rejoice! Rise above all your circumstance. Come high into the heavenly realm with Me.

Allow Me to stir up the fire inside of you. Allow My anointing to come on you super strong today. Lay all your doubt and unbelief at your feet.

Look high up to Me with praise in your mouth and songs on your heart. Let My anointing break the yokes inside of you still that would try to hold you back from coming into this higher realm in Me.

It is through your praising and your rejoicing that I the Lord your God will set you totally free. It is in your rejoicing and praise that I want to deliver the breakthroughs that you have been seeking.

Come to Me with praise and thanksgiving that I am going to start moving like never before. Praise and rejoice in Me that I am going to protect you through all the darkness that is coming your way. Rejoice in Me that you have made it to the next level in Me and that My harvest of lost souls are going to start coming in.

Those who may have heard about Me are truly going to know who I am. Those who have never heard of Me are going to have hope and a chance to have a place to join us in this heavenly realm and be brought into My kingdom. People are going to be changed with a blink of an eye. Supernatural things are going to start happen of things that you would of never thought would be possible.

My angels here in heaven rejoices for every soul that truly comes to the throne of grace and is saved; they praise and rejoice for every mind that has decided to be renewed in Me. They celebrate in the fact that I am Lord, and I will not quit loving My children and I will not allow My little sheep to be lost forever. They rejoice and celebrate when they are returned to the flock. I want My children here on Earth to praise Me as well.

Celebration came before the death of My Son because the end result was worth the celebrating. The celebration of new life and being able to be saved from sin and have a place here in heaven with Me was on the lips of My people as the praised My Son for being the King of Kings and Lord of Lords. Even though great sorrow was coming they knew the victory that was coming was so much greater than the loss and sorrow.

Yes many dark things are coming your way. Yes I want you to heed My warnings and listen to what I have instructed you. Today I do not want you to think about all this devastation that is coming your way. Those concerns can be dealt with another day. I want you to learn to praise Me no matter what is coming your way. It is through your praise and rejoicing that the darkness will not consume you.

Today I want total praise from My faithful, chosen people. The celebrations are going to have to begin in your hearts and on your mouths because they are going to very soon start breaking out all over from those who have decided to come up with Me into the heavenly realm.

Celebrations are going to come from those who have put their trust in Me and not look at what goes on around them, but puts them into My hands for Me to have complete control. You will not be burden down with all the unnecessary cares because you, My faithful children will know that I will take care of it all. Praise Me this day. Rejoice in Me and again I say rejoice!

Philippians 4:4-13
****

STAND IN THE GAP

My children, today I want you to put on your complete armor today and fight. I need My children today to intercede for each other and yourselves.

Much deception is going on, even for the ones who think they are truly following Me. I want you to fight today to have your eyes open to see into the hearts of others and yourselves.

I want you to use what you to see to go into the courtroom and the battle field and fight the enemy today like never before.

My faithful children are being deceived by thinking that some other children of mine are completely following Me, and they are not. Because My faithful children have been deceived by this they have stopped interceding for these ones they thought are ok.

My children, please fight to have your eyes opened to this, but do not let it drag you down. Let it stir up your determination to intercede for these children, these sheep who may go astray if no one intercedes.

Put on your battle gear today and fight My children for these ones to strengthen themselves in Me. Pray to have the supernatural ability to see their hearts the way that I see them, so that way the prayers and warfare is done correctly.

It is very soon harvest time. It is harvest time not just for the lost souls/sheep to come into My house, but harvest time of your blessings or your curses.

What have you sown that you will reap? If you do not fight today for others and yourselves to lift all deception then it will be more deception that you will reap.

Do not allow pride or your carnal thoughts bring you to where these other children of Mine are or to be blinded to what is really going on. This is not the mind that you have asked Me for. Do not allow the enemy to trick you into going into your old mindsets. Do not become judgmental in what is revealed to you. Use all the tools I have given you to bring them up to your level and strengthen in Me.

Deception is not of Me. Peirce this deception with prayer and with My Word that I have given you that is a double edged sword.

Do not give up fighting My children. The harvest time is right around the corner. There is a time when all that I have said will come into fruition. There is certain things and certain times that these things can happen.

The things I have promised you is ready to begin to start reaping in your life. So do not be discourage, instead fight for Me this day. Strengthen your faith in Me and know that all of these things will happen as you wait upon Me.

Have you done all the sowing and instructions that I have given you for you to reap your harvest of blessings? Are you willing today to fight for others and yourself to tell the enemy what he is not going to steal from you, including your walks with Me?

Intercede My children this day. Have your eyes opened to the truth. It is the truth that will set others and yourselves free from this deception. Become the warriors and intercessors that I have called you to be.

Many souls will depend on your decisions you make today. Put on your battle gear, your full armor in Me and take the field and My angels will be right there with you fighting right by your side and you will begin to see the results of your battle and intercession very quickly.

Who will you intercede for this day? Who are you willing to have your eyes open to and let Me show you the truth so you can go into battle for them or you? There is even ones in your family that depend on your decision today.

My judgment arm is here. I am ready to bring the full judgment on My people. Stand in the gap this day for My people, your brothers and sisters and yourselves that you may be spared from this harsh punishment that I am getting ready to bring down.

Stand in the gap to allow My harvest of souls and blessing to come forth unto My people and into My church. Fight today, My faithful children, Fight.

Galatians 6:1-10

****

DON'T COMPROMISE

Do not compromise your walk with Me. Do not take your eyes off of Me when My supernatural wonders begin in and around you.

It is I the Lord your God that will be giving the instructions to My servant Angels to come down to give you words from the books here in heaven. It is I the Lord your God that is making all things possible through Me and My Son.

Do not forget the One who is to be worshipped. Do not begin to worship the wonders and miracles. Do not allow the worship of the Angels or of the one who is the willing vessel to do what I have called them to do. This will cause you to have idols before Me.

Do not twist the words I give you. Do not add and do not take away from the things that I will be revealing to you. I am warning you this day My children so you do not fall into these traps. I am the one true God and I will be bring the supernatural and miracles gifts to the forefront.

Today, My children, get determined in Me to do what I have been calling you to do and to keep your eyes upon Me at all times. Do not correct anyone unless I have told you to do so. If they are in the wrong, I will do what I have to do to make it correct. I do not want you to for one minute act in the flesh because much damage could come out of it.

I do not want My lost sheep to be scared away because you thought you could do a job that I have not instructed you to do. I will send the one who will do the correcting the way I want it done and in the way that they will receive it.

Today I need you to worry about your walk with Me. I want you to look, reflect, and examine your walk with Me. You must stay on the straight and narrow path that I have set before you.

I want to give you, My children, much revelation from My heavenly realm, but first, today, I need you to get rid of all the things that you hold onto and will not give Me complete control. Once you give Me complete control, your stress, frustrations, anger, and all sense of overwhelming helplessness will be gone and a peace in Me will completely consume you.

It will not matter what is going on around you. It will not matter what people say to you. It will not matter how people treat you. It will not matter what the enemy brings your way. You will have the peace and understanding that all you have to do is give it to Me. Once you see, hear, or feel it, just say Lord, here it is I give it to you.

Who do you think they are really doing all this to anyways? Are you not My children and My chosen ones? Have I told you woe to be to those who come against My anointed ones? It is Me that they are coming against. It is Me that they are doing these things too.

I will not sit back and watch My children continue to be hurt. Just because you do not see immediate results does not mean that I am not causing My judgment to take place on these people who do these things.

Put all your trust in Me today. Give Me all this stress and overwhelming circumstances. Put your eyes on Me and enter My peace.

If you cannot do this, then you do not trust Me. If you do not trust Me, I cannot take care of you in this darkness. I need you My children to do these things this day. Do not tie My hands because you are holding on to the things and circumstances of this world. Give them to Me.

I want you to get to this place so I can reveal the scrolls, prophecies, and your full destinies to you. I desire for you to get to this place, so that I can perform My miracles, signs, wonders, and supernatural things through you.

Do not give up My children. This has not been for nothing. This is a promise I give to you this day.

Now do what I have instructed and enter My peace that passes all understanding and come into My heavenly realm and find your inner peace.

Revelation 22:6-11; Philippians 4:7
****

LACK FEAR OF ME

My children, I speak to you today with a heavy heart. My children, I have warned you, I have pleaded with you, I have praise you, I have encouraged you, but you still do not heed the words that I tell you.

You lack the fear of Me. Do I have to bring My wrath in all its fullness to get your attention?

Do you have to see devastation and disaster before you will see that what I have been trying to teach you that you must learn?

I am a Father that wishes to protect My children, but I cannot do that if you do not fear Me and listen to what I have instructed you to do.

Many of you, My children, tell Me you are too busy, you do not have time. You tell Me, you will do it tomorrow or when it is convenient for you.

I have warned you over and over that the time is short, but because of your lack of fear in Me, you think that I will continue to give you a grace period. The grace period is over after today.

The time has run out. My sentencing is coming forth very shortly and there will be no time to decide then to get it right.

The time is now for you to get rid of your doubt and unbelief. It is time that you find your fear of Me again. If you do not find your fear in Me again and the devastation and disaster comes, I will have a deaf ear to you during that season. I will be there by your side, but I will not be able to help you.

You will reap the things that you have sown in your idle time that you put before Me. If you do not heed My Words of instructions and do the things I have been teaching you, if you do not find your fear in Me again, you will partake in the sentencing of those who would also not heed My Words and My instructions.

I do not want any of My children to endure any of what is coming. But most of you, My children will not heed My Words. Time is out. My judgment has come down onto My people. Do not be a part of what is getting ready to take place.

Realize the seriousness in My Words. Realize the urgency in My Words. You do not have time to play around. You must completely get serious in Me. You must decide to follow Me in all the fullness. You must give up all the things that holds you back in your walk with Me.

If you call out to Me this day, and ask for the fear of Me, I will place it in your heart. I will give you grace this day and allow you this chance to get it right. There is hope, if you heed My Words this day.

Do not let this chance pass you by. If you get your fear back of Me, I can impart much more wisdom inside of you that will get you through all the devastation that is coming.

I am your Father. I do not want to see My children suffer though this tragic time that is coming. I want to see My children laughing and rejoicing that they have been spared.

Come to Me this day and ask for the fear of Me back into your lives and completely commit to Me. And I will give you the fear of Me and the hope that you will make it through all that in what is coming.

The judgment has been set. The punishment is quickly coming. Will you heed to Me this day or will you turn a deaf ear and put Me off again?

I love you, My children, with an everlasting love. But as a father loves his children, he also must chastise his children to get them on the path that they need to be on. A father must disciple those who did not listen to his voice and allow the punishment to come forth to teach the lesson that needs to be taught. I your Heavenly Father am no different.

Listen to Me this day and great will be your reward. Come to Me with true repentance in your heart, receive the fear of Me once again, and commit your ways unto Me. As you do this I will give your rest, reassurance, and comfort that I will protect you through all the darkness that is coming very soon.

I love you, My children. Do not let this chance pass you by. Heed My Words this day and come to Me.

Jeremiah 5:21-31; Proverbs 1:20-33
****

I AM YOUR PROVIDER

My children, build up your faith in Me this day.

Remember that I am the God that provided for My children when I got them released from Eygpt.

Remember that I am the God that gave Joshua direct instructions on how to tear down the walls of Jericho.

Remember that I am the God who has performed miracle after miracle for My people.

Remember that I am the God who sent My only begotten Son to this Earthly realm to suffer and die for your sins, that you, too can be reunited with Me your Father.

I am the same God today as I was back then and I have not changed. If I can provide for the birds of the air, I will provide for the ones that I have created and have breathed My breath into.

You are falling into the traps of My children that I saved from Egypt. You complain for everything you don't have. Yet your faith is so small to believe for more than you do have.

I provide things for you, and you forget as fast as they came. You decide that it is not enough. You make up your mind that I can do some things, but not all. This is not the mindset that I have instructed you to have.

You refuse to do the things that I have instructed you to do, yet you still want to receive the reward of what was promised. And when you do what I have instructed, you ask Me of things you need, but then you do not keep your faith were it needs to be to receive what you are in need of. You take it back into your own hands instead of trusting Me that I will provide it for you when the time is right. But you blame Me for not providing for you.

You have started to have a heart of complaining instead of praising Me. I have told you before, My timing is not your timing. You must put your faith and trust in Me that I am a Father that will take care of My children. You must do this thing this day.

Do not become ungrateful children. Do not become lazy and disobedient children. You will see those who you think do not have much, are very rich. You will see those who you think have a lot, are very poor.

Those who do not have much become thankful for the little they have. As they continue to praise Me for what they have, as they continue to praise Me with what they get blessed with, as they continue to use in the fullness of what they receive, their blessings will multiple because they will know that it is I the Lord their God that is doing these things for them. They give Me all the glory and all the praise.

If I make them rich in the land quickly they will soon forget the things I have done for them. There are others that are simply doing My work and great will be their reward for waiting and when the season is over.

For those who have a lot are not content with what they have. They are becoming ungrateful and full of "what about me". They come to Me complaining and letting what they do have go to waste.

Do not judge the poor and say I am not moving in their behalves or blessing them, for this is a sign that you need to seek My face and see what is dark in your heart that I need to cleanse you of before this darkness over takes this land.

Do not allow these things to hold yourself back from what I want to bless you with or keep you from My protection. Do not question the things that I am doing.

The praises of rich and judgmental, their lips have become dead because their mouths are full of self instead of praying and interceding for others.

I will not bless ungrateful and selfish children who are also disobedient and lazy. You must get your eyes off of yourself and put them on Me so I can open your eyes to the needs of others that I need you to stand in the gap for. As you do this you will then begin to see what you have, you have a lot of in Me.

You will see that I am instruction you in getting yourself right in Me so I can bless you and protect you from all things coming in the near future. I can give you more of an abundance because you will have given Me the honor and glory for all that I have given you.

You will have become grateful and ready to receive more and use it wisely. I have a work to be done and I desire to use you, but I cannot until your heart and mind is corrected.

Put praises of Me back into your hearts and allow them to flow from your lips. Become alive in Me with your praises. Get your faith and trust back into Me and know that I will provide every need as you need it. Keep it in My hands. Pray for one another and do not become self-centered.

Today allow your faith to grow more in Me that I am God and I will provide for My children. Allow your faith to grow in Me and know that I am the same God today as I always have been. Those things I have done for My other children I will do for you.

Be willing to pay the price to follow Me. Leave your needs in My hands and trust that I will do the rest. I am your father of compassion and willingness to take care of My children.

Put your faith in Me and do not waiver. Praise Me for the things I have done and going to do.

Psalm 103; James 1:17

****

A CHANGING HEART PLEASES ME

My children, your hearts are changing and in this I am pleased. Today I want you to take a rest from all the worldly circumstances. I want you to come into the heavenly realm with Me and rejoice. I want you to be renewed in Me this day.

I want your faith, joy, and love to be built stronger in you today by being in My presence. Many days of darkness are ahead. There is a lot of work yet to be done. There is much fighting in the future that I need you to get your strength back to be able to fight the good fight.

Today, I want you to be happy in Me. I want you to lay all your burdens down at My feet and find rest. Sing praises to Me this day, that I am your deliverer from darkness. Praise Me this day that I am your savior that has promised you eternal life.

Allow the joy to bubble up inside of you today. You will need this day to recuperate and make yourself strong in Me and prepare for more and stronger spiritual warfare. But do not be concerned about this today. Enjoy yourself in My presence. Sup with Me this day.

Share Me as you spend time with your family and with others today. Let them see that I am still a God who brings joy to My children's heart, laughter to their mouths, and praises on their lips. Let them see that you have everything in Me.

Plant the seed this day that you have what they are looking for, Me. Let them see that you have what they are trying to fill inside of them, Me. Show them that you do follow a loving and wonderful Father who does love His children.

Be encouraged this day, that you are going to be in My presence and showing those around you My love. You will be showing others around you that I am a Father who wants My children to be happy and have all their hearts desires according to My Word.

Enjoy yourself in Me and get the strength and rest you need. I am your Father and I am pleased with the works that has begun in your hearts. Rejoice in Me this day and be a light to all those around you and plant My seeds for a bigger harvest.

Psalms 28:7; Colossians 4:5-6
****

PROMISES COME THROUGH OBEDIENCE

My covenant that I have made to you, My children still stands today. I want you to rejoice today and seek My face, so I can show you truly what your inheritance is. You need to be made aware what I have promised you, so you will know on what to stand for, hold onto, and to know what the enemy desires to take from you. I need you to listen to Me this day for the battle of battles is coming, and you must be prepared.

My children before had faith that was strong in Me. When I told them to do something they were obedient and did it. This is what I am requiring from you today. I want you to be obedient to Me. I want you to praise Me and seek My face through all the hardships that you are facing. Keep your eyes completely on Me. I want you to do the things that I have ask you to do with all of your hearts. I want you to completely sell out to Me and use the gifts I have given you.

You have made covenants with Me, and I expect you to keep them as I have always kept mine. Renew your covenant to follow Me. Make your foundation in Me solid and in My truth. Make your foundation one of faith, love, praise, and full of My Word.

My true remnant, you may seem small, but strong you are. My children, the things that you have been through, you have allowed yourselves to become stronger than you even realize. This is why the enemy fights you so hard. He does not want you to realize just how strong you have gotten in Me.

Do not look at the numbers of the ones who stands by your sides, for I am allowing all of heaven to be with you throughout this land to protect you, guide you, and help you through these many devastations and disasters that are coming. They will fight with you when you battle the enemy. All you have to do is ask and call out, and they will be there to assist you.

Many miracles and signs and wonders I have allowed My children to preform through My name and more in My Son's name. You, My children will be doing even more than they did. All you have to do is renew your covenant with Me. You have to continue to praise Me, focus on Me and not the things of this world. You must obey the things that I have asked you to do. As you do these things My anointing, My true glory will fall like never before.

Build up your faith in Me. Remember all the things that I have save My children from in My Word. I am still the same God and I will do the same and greater for My children now. You must know and believe that I will do these things.

My judgment is here for those who have not decided to do what I have asked, but continued to do the things of this world and to stay with and desire the things of Egypt. I am done with allowing My anointed to be come against. My judgment on those who do just that is here. They will have to pay for all they have done to try to destroy

My anointed ones. My children, hold your head up high today and know that I am your God, and I will not allow the enemy to destroy you through the ones who are coming against you. Your strength is being built. You must put these things into practice and action to make them even stronger. Know that I am doing My part and I am working even when at times it cannot be seen.

There is so little time to prepare for these things that are coming. Buckle down this day and prepare yourselves with the knowledge of your inheritance and the promises I have made you. This is a key I give you to use to survive through the days ahead.

You are My faithful ones in whom I am calling this day to be obedient to My voice and prepare yourselves in these things. For just as the days of Egypt unfolded, the things on this country will unfold too. I protected My children then and brought them out, I will do the same for you. Be obedient and put your faith in Me and praise Me knowing that I am God and I fail you not.

Psalm 105

****

MY SANCTUARY A SACRET PLACE

Today I want My children to start building your protection in Me. I want you to start getting your place of peace, security, and safety in Me. Before soldiers go to war they get prepared. They are trained to know where to find safety, how to build it, and when to run into it.

I am asking you My children today to start the training of finding your safety and protection in Me. The battle of battles is coming My little ones. There is so much to do and time is running out. To begin to learn about My protection is in My sanctuary.

My sanctuary is a place of protection, a place of peace, a place where you can come and freely praise Me. It is where you should be able to come to Me freely with no worries of the outside world.

Many of My children do not appreciate My sanctuary. They have made it a tradition, a to-do on their check lists. Many of My children are watching times and putting limits on Me in My sanctuary instead of being hungry for Me and letting Me build up My children to the place they need to be.

They have become self-centered and not taking in to consideration what others in My sanctuary may need or even caring if anyone needs Me.

They have allowed My sanctuary to become just an emergency hospital instead of a real hospital that only has a part of an emergency department. They want things in a hurry and do not allow the real healing to begin. They look to My sanctuary as a place of a quick fix and then go on their merry ways. But so many of My lost sheep need more than a quick fix, they need a deep, surgical healing that is to be performed in My sanctuary.

Oh My children, you must get out of this mindset. My sanctuary is a place where My children are to go to get renewed, to get rooted further in Me, to find the peace in the mist of the storms, to minister to the lost and dying and bring them closer to Me.

It is a place where My anointing should flow and I am able to perform the works that I need to do. My sanctuary is a place to learn how to praise Me because it is through praising Me that will keep you from going under in these dark times ahead.

Oh My children, you must allow My fire to burn into you again for My Word. You must allow My fire to burn into you again to want to come into My sanctuary and become equipped with all that I have been trying to teach you.

I cannot send you out on the battle field where I need you unprepared. How can you bring others into My sanctuary with joy in your hearts, if you do not want to be there?

Today, I want you to get out of your old mindsets, and renew yourself in Me and find your desire to be in My sanctuary to praise Me. It is time for you to find where your true training grounds are and where to learn to build your protection from this darkness in this world.

Come back to your first love, My children. Praise Me today. Open your minds to receive the things that I am trying to teach you to get you through the days ahead. Find your protection in Me and start building the knowledge of how to use it. Find your joy again to come into My house.

Do not waste time, My children. You must heed My voice and learn to praise Me and come under My protection. Time is so short and much still is to be learned.

Open your ears and hearts to My voice. If you cannot learn to hear My voice clearly, how will you know what I am telling you when I am instructing you during this darkness? If you cannot open your hearts to receive My instructions this day, how will you follow them in the days ahead?

Do not get caught up in this very lonely season that some of My children will go through because they would not heed to My voice and went their own ways. Open your ears to My instructions today and ask for a reset on your desire to be in My sanctuary and truly learn to praise Me and find your protection in Me, My children. Time is truly running out.

Psalm 122; Psalm 91
****

DETERMINE TO SERVE

Today My children, I want you to truly separate yourselves from the things of this world and decide to truly follow Me no matter what. I want your total focus on Me and finding your strength, protection, and happiness in Me.

I do not want you any longer to worry about those who you have given the Word to and they have rejected you. I want you to put them in My hands and concentrate on getting yourself totally prepared for the times ahead. You must make up your mind today, that even if you are the only one left on this earth that will serve me that you will do it.

Remember My servant, Noah. He was the only man on this Earth that would serve Me and because of this I spared him. I gave him all the instructions, step by step of what to do to prepare himself for the destruction of the Earth. This is what I am trying to do for you, My children as well.

You need to become obedient to My voice and become determined to follow Me like never before and no matter what comes your way you will not be shaken.

Remember My servant, Abraham, and how he prayed for Sodom and Gomorrah to be spared if I could find a handful of people who still followed Me to spare the city. I could not find anyone who would except for Lot, so I provide him a way out before I destroyed the city.

Many of My children in My Word, you will find out that I spared them from the destruction of sin and of their enemies. I had these things put into My Word to show you how to get through times like these.

If you study My Word you will see, I gave them step by step instructions, supernaturally protected them, brought their enemies to their feet. But they obeyed what I told them to do. They kept their eyes upon Me and did not doubt My ways. I am the same God then as I am today.

You must have faith in Me that I will protect you through this darkness and destruction that is coming. But for Me to be able to protect you, you must be obedient to My voice.

You must be determined to serve Me even when you may be the only one. Find your determination in Me this day.

Keep your focus on Me and stay in My presence no matter what you are doing. Keep praise on your lips and prepare yourselves in Me to become the warriors that I have called you to be.

I cannot use soldiers that are not dedicated in Me. So make up your mind and heart today to be totally sold out to Me and make a true covenant with Me that you will serve Me no matter what.

Genesis 18:32-33; Genesis 19:29; Genesis 6:6-14; Psalm 16
****

BE PREPARED

Today I want you to prepare your hearts, minds, and walk in Me for what is ahead. Do not allow the darkness that is coming pull you in by deceiving you or causing you to fall into their ways.

There are many false prophets, false teachers, and very convincing talkers out there that will bring messages that will try to bring you doubt and unbelief on what is really going on and doubt the things that I have warned you is coming.

Today, I want you to sharpen your swords. I want you to sharpen your knowledge in Me and know that I am, who I say I am, and I will not ever change. The things that I have said will come to pass, will come to pass. You must know My Word and use it daily to be able to stand in the coming days. Get into My Word this day and learn of My ways on how to fight the enemy on all sides.

Yes you will be persecuted for My name sake. But great will be your reward for moving forward anyways.

I will be right by your side at all times. I will never leave you nor forsake you. You will know how to use the army of Angels that will be standing by waiting for the commands of My children.

Stand your grounds in Me at all costs. For it is in Me that you will be saved from the tragic events that will take place. You will have to know My Word in order to be able to protect yourself in the days ahead. You will need to know My Word in order to know what I say is true. You will need to know My Word in order to fight the battle of battles.

For in the days ahead you truly will not be fighting flesh, but principalities and powers and ruler of the darkness. You will be fighting the darkest of demons yet to have been faced. But through the knowledge of My Word and your faith in Me you will prevail in My Son's blood and by His name.

Get into My Word and prepare yourself this day. Open your spirit to My Holy Spirit and allow Him to show you the secrets and hidden weapons in My Word. Prepare yourselves, My children to get ready to take the battle field. You will be victorious in Me. But first you must be prepared for battle and for the victory.

2 Timothy 3
****

COME IN MY PRESENCE

Come into My presence this day. Come into My presence this day and truly worship Me. Come into My presence this day and sit with Me. Let Me just spend time with you. Let Me engulf you with My love. Let Me fill you with My peace.

As you truly worship Me, you will feel yourself be renewed again with My Spirit. You will begin to feel the fire start burning inside again for My Word and My ways. I desire to spend time with you this day.

I desire to sup with you and just to be with you. I want to comfort you and hold you. I want to bring you into this heavenly place. I want you to feel My presence. I want you to get a taste of the Holy of Holies.

Slow down today and spend time with Me, My children. I want some alone time with you to show you just how much I love you. I desire you to worship Me and show Me how much you love Me.

Spend time with Me today and just see what I do to you. Spend time with Me today and see what I show you.

This is what I desire from you, My children this day. All I desire from you is to come into My presence and spend time with Me.

Romans 12:1; Hebrews 13:15; John 4:23-24
****

SURRENDER IN PRAISE

I want you to come into My presence. I want you to allow Me to give you the overhaul change that you are in need of. There are many things that you, My children need, but first, you need a recharge in Me.

I see the weariness and the questions. But I need you to get into My presence so I can take care of these concerns and comfort you that I am in full and complete control.

The only way to get this is to come into My presence and spend time with Me. As you worship, you open your hearts to Me to allow Me to change and rearrange the things that need to be done inside of you.

You need to allow Me to give you a brand new mindset. A mindset of My heavenly realm and not of one of this world. With the mindset you have now, you will not be able to handle the supernatural things that I am about to do. Because some of you have not keep your eyes on Me and have begin to look at the situations and circumstances around you, you have started to fall into despair, hopeless, and defeat.

I am asking you today to get your eyes back on Me and keep them there. Come into My presence and let Me supercharge you with My anointing.

Allow Me to do the works. Let Me fill you with My love so you can share it with the world. If you cannot feel My love and know that I love you, how are you going to convince others to come to Me and let Me find them completely and tell them that I love them from the depths of your hearts? You cannot do this thing if you do not believe it yourself.

You must get into My presence and let Me renew you. Raise your hands in surrender to Me. Let Me show you just how much I truly do love you, My children. Let Me show you My secrets that I want to reveal to you. Oh, My children, I long to spend time with you. The hour is late and there is so little time to finish the works that have only just begun in some of you.

Come into My presence this day and truly step into My love and watch the wonderful things that I will start doing and showing you in your life. Come into My presence with true worship in your hearts and praise on your lips. Come into the safety of My arms and know that I am a Father who loves My children.

Come to Me today and enter into My presence. Let Me revive the thirst for Me again. Let Me renew your desire of Me once again. Let Me show you that I am still the God who true does love My children.

Jeremiah 29:10-14; Psalm 42
****

CONTINOUS DISOBEDIENCE EQUALS NO GRACE

My children, I see the questions in your hearts about the things that you have heard and are starting to see. I have been giving you answers to some of these questions, but many of you do not want to hear them.

Yes, I am full of grace and you cannot earn grace, but it is a gift that I give. But there does come a time when My grace runs out.

My children you must understand that My grace has run out on those who have chosen to be disobedient to My voice. You must understand that I truly do not want anyone to be punished and go to hell, that is why I allowed My Son to come to this Earth and die for everyone to have a way out to come to Me here in heaven.

But so many have decided to turn their backs on Me and serve satan. They have rejected Me and have allowed themselves to be ruled by him. I cannot allow grace on those who have turned their backs on what I have done for them and allow them to dishonor My Son's blood.

My grace is here for those who have yet to turn their backs on Me. My grace is here to those who have not heard My Word or had the chance to decide to truly follow Me. My grace is here for those who are truly following Me. But My grace is gone to those who have turned away from Me and have not heeded My voice.

I will protect you, My children, who have truly decided to follow Me and to do the works that I need done here on Earth. You need to continue to get into My presence and find the peace that I have for you. You need to put on the armor that I have given to you daily and use the Word that I have provided for you. This will get you through this terrible season ahead.

You must understand that you will be in your prayer closets constantly and will have to know when to intercede and when not to.

You can only know this if you are in tuned to My voice and hear the things that I am telling you and follow instructions.

I am asking you today to make up your mind to keep moving forward in Me no matter what is going on around you. I am asking you today to make up your mind to trust Me 100% that I am a God that is justice and loving.

Today, I want you to come into My presence and let Me wrap My arms around you and let you feel the comfort that only I can bring.

I understand the questions and the concerns and soon most things you will come to understand, some you will not. Remember My ways are not your ways, but I know what I am doing. I am a God who is trying everything I can to save My children, but it is up to them to want to be saved.

Come to Me today for comfort, reassurance, love, and peace.

Come to Me today, and let Me help renew the mind to understand that there are some things that has to happen in attempts to get the attentions of those who I want to save.

Come to Me and allow Me to do a work on your mind to truly trust Me and know that I am God and I will protect and take care of My children.

Deuteronomy 11:26-28; Isaiah 3:1-11

****

RECEIVE MY LOVE TO LOVE EVERYONE

Today is a day that I want you to love. Love those around you that seem so impossible to love. I want you today to get this in your spirit and make it a part of your mind. You need to get the love of My son inside your heart.

The problem, My children, is you lack your love for Me, so having the love of My Son has been almost an impossible task. You need to build your love in and for Me. My love is not one of this world.

My love is one that does not try to see what is gained for self. No, My love is unconditional with no limitations and never ends regardless if I get it back. Even when My children disobey Me and turn their backs on Me, I still love them. Even when souls go to hell, I still weep over them and love them despite what they have done to get there. Love does not have an end just because you have done wrong or you do not receive it back.

Is it going to be easy? NO. If it was easy, everyone would be able to do it. If everyone would love the way that My Son and I love, there would be so much love in this world that sin would not be able to abide. Is love powerful? Absolutely.

The love of My Son and I is so powerful that it breaks yokes, heals broken hearts, holds those who are hopeless, feeds those who are starving-physically and spiritually, forgives those who does wrong to us and hurt My children, and the list goes on.

Do I get angry? Yes, I get angry with disobedience and hatred and sin. Yes, I punish the wrong, but I never stop loving them.

In this darkness that is coming, true pure love is going to be so hard to find. But I require My children to have it and give it. It is My second greatest commandment of you. You must love each other. It will be the only thing that will be able to keep My harvest in the church and to follow Me. It will be what draws them and keeps them. It is the greatest medicine that you can give to the lost and dying and those who are hurt and wounded.

You must reflect My love in order for them to have an idea of how much I love them. Yes, the miracles, signs, and wonders may get their attentions, but it will be the love that you have that will truly bring them to their knees at the cross. It is at the cross where they need to be to be saved. It is only through My Son that you can come to Me.

I want you to come into My presence today and allow Me to start depositing this love into your hearts today. I want you to learn to love Me as I love you. I want you to learn to love others as I love you. As you learn to do this, you will have a brand new perspective on your life. You will see that things will come easier to you. Yes, this is a hard task that I am asking of you, but I am requiring you to do this. You must learn to love.

If you cannot love My Son or Me, then you cannot make heaven your home. If you cannot love one another, you do not love My Son or Me. Today, you must begin your walk of true, pure love that comes from My Son and Me and My heavenly place.

Come into My presence and let Me inject your heart with it this day and begin to truly see My love and feel it for what it truly is.

Get into My Word and study it. See how love prevailed over and over. See how those who did not show love would fall. Love is one of the most powerful tools that you can carry. Come to Me today and allow Me to begin this love walk in you.

Matthew 22:36-39; Ephesian 3:14-21; John 14:6
****

COME AWAY WITH ME TO THE MOUNTAIN TOP

Today, I want a date with My children. I want you to come onto the mountain top and spend time with Me. I want to rekindle the love that you had for Me the day that I found you, and you decided you wanted to be saved from the wickedness of the world. Oh how I miss the time that we spent together. I so desire to stir up that fire again inside of you for the things of Me and of My ways.

You have become children that only want Me in your lives when you think you need Me. But I am letting you know today that you need to have a relationship with Me at all times.

You have become children who think that your wisdom is all you need and once you have made your mistakes and ran out of options then you come to Me. Because I love you so much you were able to do this and I would be right there to fix them.

I need to listen closely to Me today, My children. There is no more room to go off on sprees and make wild and careless mistakes. The times have gotten too dark and time has ran out. If you do not learn to have Me in your life at all times and allow Me to put My wisdom into your hearts and minds and follow it, then your mistakes will cause you great punishment and may even cause you death.

I do not want this for you My children. I do not want to see you go to the way side. However, I will not go against your will. I have warned you over and over about what is here and what more is soon to come. I have been giving you the tools you need to fight and stay on top. I have many more plans that I want to do with you, but first I need you to come back to your desire to follow Me and love Me the way you first loved Me.

I want to show you just how much I still love you and desire to be with you. I am standing at the mountain top waiting to see who will come up here with Me. I have much to share with My children, but I am only going to reveal My secrets to those who will come back to their pure love in Me. I will only reveal My secrets to those who will die out to their flesh and spend quality time with Me.

Even though there is much darkness and devastation coming, even though there will be much sorrow and pain for those who chose not to listen to Me, I want you to know there is also a season of blessings that is getting ready to pour out on My faithful children. It will be blessings upon blessings, more than you could imagine. It will be blessings that will make going through these terrible times easier than it will be for others.

I will take care of My children just as I always have. I have things that are lining up and make things just so. I am doing this so that way the enemy cannot have a foot to stand on to take My blessings that I give you this time away from you. Be patient and know that I am God and I will do all that I said I would do.

For now, come to the mountain tops with Me. Rekindle your love and your fire to serve Me. Spend some time in My presence and just let Me wrap you in a blanket of My love. And when you come down you will be able to share this love with everyone around you. Come on this date with Me today and watch the rest of your life change.

I love you My children and I am waiting. Will you be one of the ones who will come to the mountain top date with Me?

Exodus 19:3-6; Deuteronomy 5:4; Luke 9:28-29;
1 Kings 19:11-12; Numbers 6:24-26
****

PRAY MY WILL

Many around you, My children, are speaking things into existence. There are things that it is not time to come to pass, but My children are not interceding to stop these things from happening. They are allowing the things to be said and are listening to the lies and deceit. There are people speaking things into your lives personally, spiritually, and in your land.

My faithful children, turn your eyes and ears to Me this day and hear My voice. A select few knows what is going on and what people are trying to do. I have given this wisdom to them so you will know how to pray, when to pray, and what to pray for. But so many of My children are not praying. If you do not start interceding today, the devastation will be worse than it was intended to be at this time.

Yes, I am telling you what is going to happen before it does, so you can get yourselves prepared in Me. Yes, I will keep you supernaturally safe because you are here to do a works for Me during these times.

Yes, much devastation is coming, but there is so many things going on behind the scenes that the enemy would like to do more to destroy My people. Because of the words that goes into the air and no one is interceding for the curses and destruction that they are speaking and believing in existence, I will have to let it happen.

I am asking you this day to start interceding for My will at this time. Start interceding for the safety of My children and your families. It is only through prayer, intercession, and praise that you will get through this. You must pull yourselves together and pray. This is where unity comes into play.

Do you not understand that the enemy is working full force to get the antichrist to come forth before it's time? Do you not understand that the enemy is not letting up and is going to continue to push forward and at this point there has been very little resistance?

Make up your mind this day to fight. Yes, I know the enemy is fighting you in your personal lives. But I am here with My army to fight your battles.

Give your battles to Me and intercede now for My will to be done, so I can intervene at this time. I need you to become the soldiers I have been training you to be.

It is time to pick up your swords today and put a stop to the enemies plans. Fight My children. Fight for My kingdom and Fight for My will to be done. Fight with the tools I have given you.

If you will only praise Me and see just how powerful praise truly is, My children. If you cannot find the words to say, or you feel like you are stuck in the battle and don't know which way to turn-praise Me.

My angels will be with you during this battle time if you ask for them. My Holy Spirit will be upon you, if you invite Him to be there. My Son will be there to intercede on your behalf of warfare and interceding for My will as long as you bring Him with you. So put on your armor today, My children, and fight.

The victory is already yours, so fight for it this day. Show the enemy that you are My children and you will not tolerate what he is trying to do. And then see how I will show up and let them know that I am your God and I will not fail you.

Psalm 52
****

ARM YOURSELF WITH THE ARMOR OF GOD

Today, My children, I want you to truly and completely cloth yourselves in the armor that I have given you. I want you to get completely prepared to battle the enemy. Get your swords sharpened, your helmet strengthen, and make sure that your armor fits the way it is made to fit.

Without My armor you are very venerable to allowing the enemy to come in like a flood and bring fear into your life. He will use this fear to destroy you and bring you away from Me.

Now is not the time to let your guard down. With the devastation and destruction that is coming, he will use fear to pull you under. Put on My armor that I have given you to protect yourself from him and to be able to go into the battles that are before you and know that I, your Father, will keep you safe and will be with you at all times.

I want you to understand that it is time to start fighting in the spirit more than ever and even in new ways. It is time to start putting the tools that I have taught you into fruition and stand on the solid foundation that you have been building in Me.

It is time to take action in your prayer closets and truly go into battle and truly use all that you have been given instead of just excepting things or giving up or expecting others to do it for you. You must fight for your own salvation, safety, and walk in Me.

You must close all doors to your doubt and unbelief and allow your faith in Me to completely take over. You do not have any room for doubt or unbelief that you will do all that I said you will do in My name and My Son's or it will cause you to fall.

You must know who you are in Me. You cannot attach yourself onto someone else and expect them to carry you anymore. You have been given the tools and the instructions. It is time for you to use them yourself. Your strength is in Me not in another.

You must get your mind completely renewed and made like My Son's. Your mind is where the enemy fight you the most. This is why I have given you a helmet of salvation. Because My Son's blood the enemy cannot penetrate or destroy.

Your mouth is what the enemy will use against you trying to destroy you with your words and if you do not get your mind renewed your thoughts will come out of your mouth and the enemy will be there to use them against you.

Your thoughts cannot be ones of this world. You must stay focused on Me and of the spiritual things. You cannot be wondering or pondering on what others are doing and getting away with or wanting to see what you can get away with. You cannot judge or condemn others for their wrong doings.

Trust Me, My children I do see and My judgment is here and will be coming to pass very shortly. This is why I need you to have your eyes and ears open to My voice so you will know when to intercede, when to put it in My hands and leave it alone, and when to shake off the dust and move on and what will be done, will be done.

You must completely die out to all your sin nature. Die out to your flesh daily and invite the Holy Spirit to be manifested in you every day. Ask for My Son's light to be shown that you will be a true vessel that I can work through.

Yes, you are all sinners and come short of My glory, but that is why I gave the sacrifice of My Son; to be used to cleanse and purify you to make you righteous in My eyes. Use this thing that I am telling you against the enemy. Do not give into his lies.

As you put on My armor, you will be able to see through the enemy's lies that he tries to feed you every day. Really get to know what is My armor and why it is there for you to use.

Do not let it become dusty and bagged up and become unused. Put it on daily, polish it up, and strengthen it in Me and in My Word and through your praises and worship to Me.

Allow Me today to show you the full use of My armor. Allow Me to further your armor in Me by allowing Me to do more work on you. I want to remove the blinders and cloudy vision from your eyes. So you can see where you are going and which path to take to victory.

I want to unclog and open your spiritual ears to hear My voice and not question if it is Me. You will have to be able to hear My instructions on when to stay still, when to battle, when to run, and when to move forward.

I want you to allow Me to cleanse your mouths that they will only speak of My truth. I want you to allow Me to open your hearts to truly understand what is going on and not by what is going on not just in the natural realm, but what is truly going on in the spiritual realm.

The things you see here on this earth are really things that are going on in the spiritual realm because the evil has been allowed to manifest itself. You will not be able to survive or fight with earthly things. You will only be able to survive and fight with what I have been training you with and been giving you to use.

Many are looking at the flesh that is bringing these things forth and that is what will cause many to fall. But My children, you must understand this is a spiritual thing because it will be the only way you can keep a heart of compassion to want to bring the soul to Me.

You must allow Me to open the heart and allow Me to love through you because if you only use your understanding and looking at the natural your heart will become bitter and hatred towards the person and not want to do what I have called you to do, which is to bring these souls to the cross.

Today, My children, put on the armor that I have given you. Allow Me to give you the extended armor of new eyes to see, new ears to hear, a mouth that is cleansed, and a new heart that is open for Me to use.

As you do this you will start to see and understand more clearly the things that I have been telling you and instructing you to do. It's time to start fighting,

My children. Fight with what you have been given so far. But also know that I will be giving you more in the very short seasons ahead.

There is no more looking back or moving backwards. It's time to march and move forward.

Take My hand this day and allow Me to do these works that I need to do on you. And always make sure you are clothed in My armor that I have given to you and come to understanding on how to use it.

2 Kings 6:17; Ephesians 1:18; Psalms 141:3;
Numbers 22:38; Revelation 3:22; Ephesians 6:10-18
****

ROOT YOUR FAITH IN ME (PART 1)

What does your faith allow you to believe for today? My children, I want you to examine your faith in Me. You must get all your doubt and unbelief pushed far away from you and have your mind renewed completely and fully in Me. I have asked you to be yes people. I heard the yes from My faithful people that answered when I called.

So what does a yes person mean … obedience. I need you to obey My voice, My calling, and do what I say to do no matter what. It will take great faith and obedience to do some of the things that I have called some of you to do.

Remember My ways are not your ways and My thoughts are not your thoughts. But as you line up your ways and thoughts with My Word, your faith will build and your obedience will become sharper and quicken to My voice and when I call.

I want you to know where you stand and exactly what can you believe Me for and what I can do for you and with you. I need My children to have the faith to raise the dead, heal the sick, set the captives free, know that I will provide for them when there is no food or water to be found, to know that I am doing all that I said I will do. So where does your faith lie today?

Many of My children only has a small amount of faith and I need them to water their seed quickly and grow that seed so I can use them, protect them, and allow My miracles, signs, and wonders flow through My children and bring in My harvest.

I desire that you get your faith rooted and grounded firmly in Me because what I am going to use My children for in this next seasons ahead will require faith. You must know where you are at with Me because people will know if you believe what you proclaim or if you are just blowing hot air and saying something that has been drilled in you.

How far you go in Me will require faith. How much you will accomplish fighting and surviving will require faith. There is no room for doubt and unbelief. I want you today to get rid of it and get your faith growing fast.

When soldiers go to war they have faith that they will win and the victory is theirs. I need My soldiers to have the same mindset. The battles you are facing right now are training battles for what is ahead.

So get your faith built strong in Me and use your faith to fight the battles. It is not resting time anymore. Your battles will get harder and stronger and I will be right here with you to provide you with the tools that you will need as the battles grow. But it requires faith to know that through Me all things are possible, you already have the victory, and that I am a God that will do what I said I will do.

Go back into the words that I have given you and see where I have given you the instructions of what to do and what to prepare for in the days and seasons ahead. If you have not done what I have instructed you to do, do them. If you have not prepared for what I have told you to prepare for then get prepared.

Go through your notes that you have taken and the lessons you have learned. I have been getting you ready for what you are about to face, but have you been paying attention? There is so little time left before the major destruction hits.

Have you been allowing your faith to grow, your eyes to be opened, your ears in tuned to My voice, your heart opened and filled with My love, your mind lined up with My ways and My thoughts, your mouth cleansed and filled with My Words? Ask yourself these questions this day and work on where you lack. Build up your faith My children. There is only a window of opportunity to get this right. What will you believe for and how far will your faith in Me take you?

Matthew 17:19-20; Matthew 21:21-22; Hebrews 11; Hebrews 12:1-3
****

TRUE LOVE (PART 2)

My children, today I am asking you to do part 2 of what I asked you yesterday. I want you to examine your love walk. I want you to ask yourself... Do I love everyone the way that Jesus loved Me? Do I love everyone the way that my Father loves Me? I want you to open your heart today and really examine what is in there.

I need you to have My love. My love is full of compassion, forgiveness, grace, and mercy. My love is also full of discipline, expectations from My children, justice, and peace. Yes, My love is hard at times. But if I did not love you at all times and in all ways would you truly straighten up and follow Me?

My children you must understand that as a Father I must chastise those who I love because if I did not then I could not say I love you. I cannot allow you to fall behind and sit back and do nothing.

What is your definition of love today? I want you to get into My Word and get the true definition of love and what I require from you this day. To make your faith strong and count, you must love.

I am not talking about when things are easy and when someone loves you back. I am also talking about those who mistreat, lash out, sin, and who does not love you. To love them you must be obedient to My voice and do what I tell you to do at the right time to show them the proper love.

For it is those who are lost and dying who needs your love through Me the most. But if you cannot love, how can you bring in the lost souls? How can you believe and expect Me to honor your faith if you cannot love which is My greatest commandment? You need this tool at all times.

I am requiring you to love. I want to bring in My harvest and without love I cannot do that. I refuse to allow them to come into My house and be destroyed from judgment and ridicule. If you cannot get your love walk under control, I will remove you from My house. I do not desire to do this thing, but there is so little time and you have had so many warnings. I have a work that needs to be done, and I have given chances after chances.

Ask Me this day to feel and know My heart and know what true love is. Very few of My children have asked for this. Very few children of Mine have decided that they must do 100% of what I have asked. I have commanded you to love, and you must keep My commandments. Join this few today and ask for a new heart in Me.

I have many things that I need to accomplish in this hour and I need you today to examine your love walk. For it is through your love walk and your faith that the true miracles, signs, wonders, and lost souls can begin.

Heed My voice today and do this of what I ask. Allow Me to change the heart and show you how to truly love through Me. Allow Me to give you a new heart.

Galatians 5:6; 1 Corinthians 13:2; Hebrews 12:6; 1 John 4:8
****

POSITION OF A SOLDIER

Today, My children, I am asking you to get yourselves into the reserves position of a soldier. I need you to be on call at this given time. I need you to be prepared and armed for battle at any given time. I need you to be prepared to be called into the battle of battles and stand in the gap for those of My children that may need you.

The battles are here, some are stronger than others. The battles that are here are designed to take My chosen ones out. The enemy will stop at nothing to accomplish this task. I need you to be on call to go into intercessory prayer at any time to stand in the gap for one another. As My children, you must fight for each other as well as yourselves.

This is not the time to try to fight alone. I have been trying to get all of My children in unity for such a time as this. When soldiers go into battle, they have to fight together not against each other and My soldiers are not different.

Things are going to come at you when you least expect it and the same goes for all of My children. Do not let your guard down with the enemy, and do not open the door for him to find an entry way into your lives to cause destruction. If you feel these things happening come into My presence, into My arms, and ask for Me to help you. Call on one another to pull each other up, for all become weak at one point or another. In numbers, you are stronger. I am giving all My faithful children the anointing to fight.

I am getting ready to move in a mighty way. I am getting My things in order and it is time to bring in My harvest. The enemy knows what is coming and his time is very short. He is going to fight even harder to take you out, My children. He will try to bombard you at all sides to wear you down.

Do not take your eyes off of Me. I am here right by your side. Remember all that I have taught you and know that I will not leave you nor forsake you.

I have legions of angels ready to fight the battles with you here in the heavenly realm and there in the earthly realm. But I am asking you My children to be on call where you are at all times. I need you in tune to My voice and walking in My Holy Spirit so that when I need to call on you that you will be able to battle no matter where you are. It is time to take what I have been teaching you and putting it into action.

Do not be discouraged or dismayed. I have called all of you, My faithful servants, for a time such as this. I have been preparing you for this. You are strong in Me and when you feel weak pull more strength from Me. Do not allow the enemy to succeed in his task.

You told Me you will do My will at all cost and I am reminding you of this to give you strength to continue to fight the good fight. Your salvation must be fought out daily. You must keep all the doors shut to the enemy. You must keep your ears and eyes open to all the attacks of the enemy and be prepared to fight. But do not fear or doubt. Stay in My peace and know you will always be in My safety because I will be right here by your side through all of this.

Hold your head high this day and be prepared to go into battle at all times. It is time to be in the reserves waiting for My call to go into battle. This I ask of you this day. And as you are waiting, strengthen yourself and others in Me and praise Me for the victory is already yours and all you have to do is stay strong and know that you have already won.

2 Chronicles 20:15-19; Joshua 10:7-8, 25; Psalms 91:11
****

ELIJAH ANOINTING

Today, I want you to learn about and ask for the Elijah anointing. This is a tool that I am giving you today to help you through the times ahead. I need you to have the boldness, determination, obedience, faith, and the closeness with Me that My servant, Elijah had.

I am willing to give you this anointing a mantle to you this day. But first, you must study and understand what you are asking for and come to Me ready to pay the price to carry such an anointing. With this anointing, comes much responsibility, but also, comes great favor and a deeper walk with Me that you have not tapped into yet, My children. It will give you a new understanding on fighting in the spiritual realm.

Study about My servant, Elijah, and know that I will do the same with you, and I will do even greater things through you. It is time to really prepare the people for My Son's second coming and for My kingdom, and bring in the harvest of lost souls.

It is time that My signs, miracles, and wonders come forth. It is time to bring forth My Word and allow the people to choose whom will they serve.

It is time to know where you stand in Me and being bold enough to show others no matter what they think about it, do exactly what I tell you to do, and know that I will be there to do what I said I will do.

It is time to stand up to the jezebels and ahabs of this time. It is time for you to have your eyes completely open to what is going on in the spiritual realm at all times. It is time to bring forth your destiny in Me that I have been calling you to step into in this hour.

This will be an anointing like no other that you have ever experienced or known. You will be able to see and know deeper and greater things than you have known. You will be able to bring them to the people and teach them of these new things that you will discover because with this anointing comes uncovered eyes and a new understanding.

I am willing to give you this anointing this day, but make sure you study about this anointing and know that it is what you are willing to have. Make sure that you are ready to walk into this anointing that I am giving you.

This is a precious thing that I want to do for you today. This is a serious anointing to have. Do not take this tool that I am giving you today lightly. Get into My Word and allow the Holy Spirit to truly show you what comes with this anointing, and if you want this anointing and you will receive the mantle, come to Me, and I will give it to you.

Read 1 Kings 17 through 2 Kings 2:18; Luke 1:16-17
****

GETTING YOURSELF IN ORDER

Today, My children, I need you to get yourselves and your business in order. I need you to get yourselves prepared to walk in My full anointing that I have called you to walk in. I am lining up all the things that I am to get in order, and you need to be doing the same.

No more procrastinating. There are things that you have told Me you would do. Do them. There are things that you will need to do now because you will not have time to do them in the near days ahead.

Come and seek My face if you do not know what you are suppose to be doing. But many of you, My children already know what you need to be doing and getting done. There is no more time to slack off.

You do not fully understand just how busy you will become as you step into the fullness of My anointing. Do not continue to put these things off.

Sit down with something to write with and make a list of things that you have said that you would do for Me. Then make a list of things that you have told others you would do that is in My will. You need to get them prioritized and start getting them done. The time for dragging your feet is over. You need to do this that I am telling you to do.

Be obedient to My voice this day. The time is do near for the things that you have been wanting to happen to come to the forefront, but you are truly not prepared with having all your things lined up the way it needs to be.

Get your worldly business in order. Get your spiritual walk in order. Do the things that I have already asked you to do and get prepared to do the things that I have told you that I am calling you to do.

You will be fulfilling your destinies, and it is coming forth. Some of you will be writing. Some of you will be learning music. Some of you will be traveling. Some of you will be waking up getting direction from Me to go to a certain place and just start ministering. Some of you will be getting up and going where I tell you to so I can perform My signs, miracles, and wonders. Some of you will be coming up here into the heavenly and being filled with much wisdom and knowledge to be brought down to others. Some of you will be going to preach My Word full time.

Whatever I have told you that you will do, that you will do. You must understand the urgency of getting these things done. You need to get done all the things so you will be completely free to do what I will be asking you to do.

Yes, not only will you need to do these things because of My mighty move that is coming but also because of the darkness that fast approaching. So many of you, My children, are not prepared, and I am calling you today to get prepared. A few of you are prepared for the majority of things in your life, but there are a few little things that still need to be done. I am willing to show you today that it needs to be done.

Please understand My children, that this needs to be done now for the window of opportunity to get this done is very small. Your walk and calling is a step by step thing. I am getting all My steps in order for you and doing what I have told you I would do. You need to be doing also getting your steps in order and doing what you have said you would do.

Seek My face this day. Bring your writing utensils with you and let's make the lists together. I will show what you need to do. Do not waste time doing them. But get them done for time and this opportunity is very short. I am waiting to hear from you, My children. It is time to get things in order.

Psalms 32:8; Proverbs 13:4; 2 Corinthians 8:10-12; 2 Timothy 4:2; John 14:12; Matthew 5:14-16
****

PRAISE IN THE MIDST OF BATTLE

Today, My children, I want you to praise Me in the midst of your battles. I want you to have praise on your lips and songs in your heart. Do not fall in the pity parties that the enemy wants you to be in. If the enemy can get you to a place of despair and discouragement he will have stolen your victory. Do not allow him to do this.

Praise Me with all of your heart. Praise Me that I am in the storm with you and I am calming the storm, so that you can get back on your feet. Praise Me that all is well.

As you praise Me you defeat the enemy. As you praise Me you are using a very powerful weapon and letting the enemy know he will not win. You are letting the enemy know that you will follow Me at all costs. As you praise Me you are hurting the enemy's ears because he knows that if you are praising Me you are not listening to him.

Get your minds off your circumstances and praise Me. Praise Me for all that I have promised you. Praise Me that I Am; and will do what I said I will do. Praise Me that you have the victory over all that is going on in your life. Praise Me.

Sing love songs to Me and just come into My presence and be strengthened and encouraged this day. Oh how I want to hear you, My children, tell Me that you love Me. I want to hear how you feel about Me. I want to know that you truly want to serve Me and want to come to the heavenly realms with Me.

Oh how I love to hear your praises. I love to hear the melodies of your heart. I love to hear the sweet and soft words off your lips. It brings such joy to Me to hear your praises.

As you praise Me the joy will start bubbling over again inside of you. As you praise Me your happiness will be restored. As you praise Me from your heart, you are allowing Me to perform miracles in your life, healing your heart, and allowing Me to fertilize the love inside of you.

Oh, My children, do you not see how powerful the praises are that come from you because you are My children? Your praises bring life into your lives and to the lives of others. It brings the positive into your life that it will no longer allow you to focus on the negative. It will keep your eyes upon Me and not at what is going on around you.

It is through your praise that you will give Me the glory and show the world just how wonderful it is to follow Me and to make heaven their home. Through your praises you will draw in the harvest of lost souls back into My arms.

Praise Me today and see what will happen to you. You will notice the difference in yourself. You will feel the love, peace, happiness, joy, restoration, and so many other things that you are in desperate need of. Strengthen yourself in Me in the midst of your battles through praise. Praises bring forth growth and help your soul prosper in Me.

Try it today and see that what I am telling you is the truth. Praise Me with your true heart and watch your faith multiply more than you would imagine. Praise Me and allow these things to take place in your life and know that My presence is there with you. You will know that I am God, and I want My children to be happy.

Praise Me this day and bring much joy to My heart and watch it transform your life into something more than you thought it was and watch what I will do.

Just praise Me today for all that I have done, am doing, and going to do.

Ephesians 2:4-10; 1 Thessalonians 5:16-18; Hebrews 13:15-16
****

KEEP PUSHING ON

My children, today, I want you to be encouraged in Me. I want you to continue to persevere through your walk with Me. Do not give up on My ways or what I have told you I will do.

I am coming to your aid. I am here to protect you, guide you, and to be with you. I have not forgotten all that I have promised. I have not turned My back on My faithful servants. I see the needs, and I desire to take care of those needs. I see the longing of the hearts, and I desire to fulfill those desires. I will do all that I said I will do, but in some promises there is a time table that has to take place so do not give up on what I have promised you.

Yes, My children, the hour is a dark hour and much devastation and darkness is still ahead. But through all of it I will be with you. Through all of it I will be the one who will cover you in a blanket of protection. I will be there to take care of all your needs and to be there as you do the works that I have called you to do.

You need to know this and believe this for the enemy desires for you to give up. The enemy wants you to doubt My promises and turn the other way. Do not allow yourself to believe his lies. There is so much that lies ahead of you.

Do not become weary and saddened for what is coming ahead. Know that I tell you and warn you ahead of time of the things that is coming to prepare you and to get you ready for what I have called you to do.

My judgment must come and has been set, but I will take care of those who keep their eyes upon Me. Keep holding on a little longer. Keep holding on to My hand a little tighter and do not let go.

There is still work that I need to do in this hour to get My faithful children ready for what is coming ahead. Allow Me to do this work in you. Allow Me to open your eyes to see what I am doing. Be patient in this time and do not grow weary in well doing. I have not

110

left you. I love you, My children. Do you not understand that in order for some of My promises to come forth I must have certain things in order?

There are some of My children who are dragging their feet in what I have asked them to do. I have been placing things in their path to speed them up to get them to do what I have asked them to do. Because of this there has been a delay in bringing forth some of My promises. But know this My faithful children, know that I will give My children the opportunity to do what I have asked until they disobey and do not repent.

I will try to nudge them onto My straight path. It is not My desire that any of My children should fall or turn away. But I cannot wait much longer for those who are dragging their feet because it is causing much discouragement and lack of hope. If they do not start picking up the slack, I must find another way to get My works done and the promises to come forth. I will not go against their will, but I have been giving them opportunities to change their minds. Be patient just a little longer My children for their souls are in jeopardy.

Pray for one another for strength, encouragement, and for obedience today. Pray for those who are dragging their feet in what I have asked them to do for there is not much time for them to wake up. Be encouraged this day that I am moving on your behalves, and I am right here with you at all times. Hold on to My hand and do not let go.

Turn your ears from the enemy, and do not allow him to continue to open doors in your life to work against you. The enemy's main goal in this hour is to take out My faithful children. My chosen people are under so much attack, but I am telling you this day that I am here to instruct you on how to fight, when to fight, and when to call for help.

I have My angels standing, ready, willing, and able to fight right beside you and for you. I am giving you the tools to be successful and victorious in these battles that you are facing.

Keep persevering in your walk with Me. Keep holding on to My hand and trusting Me this day. For all that I said will come to pass shall come to pass.

Do not keep your eyes solely on what is unfolding around you because as the devastation is coming so are My signs, miracles, and wonders. Be encouraged and strengthened in Me.

Know that I am God and I will not lie. I am a just God and I am a protector of My children. Listen to My voice and My voice only.

Do not give into the lies that are trying to take you off course with Me, but persevere through this time and be encouraged that all is well no matter what the eyes see and that I will do all that I promised I will do.

Psalms 46:1-3; James 1:2-4; James 1:12; Galatians 6:9;
Ecclesiastes 4:9-12; Ephesians 6:18
****

BECOME A TRUE SERVANT

Today, My children, I want you to become true servants. I want you to be true servants to Me, My Word, your calling I have on your life, and to each other. You need to have a true servant's heart in this hour. You need a heart that is obedient to Me to do what I have asked you to do when I have asked you to do it.

You need a heart to love when I ask you to love and not when you feel like it. You cannot decide when it is ok to love and when it is not ok. You must love at all times unless I tell you to shake the dust off your feet and keep going. But that does not mean quit loving them as a soul, it just means that your time needs to be steered onto someone or something else because the time on them is up for you.

To have a servant's heart, you must be completely sold out to Me and have your mind renewed. You cannot be a true servant and have the mind of this world. You must have the mind of My Son and of My ways. You cannot go by your understanding and ways because there will be many times you will not understand what I am doing or asking, but you must be obedient when I tell you to do what I have told you to do no matter what and no matter what the cost.

To be a true servant means, you do things according to My Word for one another without complaining and with a joyful heart. Many of My children lack in this area. I am asking you today to come to Me, so I can fix this inside of you.

Many of My children are putting down others and hurting others because they are allowing their own opinions and feelings to get in the way of what I am trying to do. You cannot continue to tear each other down anymore. If you see a problem, it is to be prayed about. And if you are having a hard time praying about it, admit it and ask someone that you know will be able to help pray about it. Or just simply ask Me to help you in this area.

How can I heal someone or bring them to Me if you are wounding them and causing them to turn away? I am a God that heals wounded hearts; not batter them more and if you are causing the battering then you are not being a true example of Me. When and if this happens or already has happened, let what I am saying be brought to your attention that you still need work on your love walk and servanthood in Me. And correct these things in Me quickly for there is no time to slack.

To be a true servant is to do things regardless if you want to do them or understand why you are being asked to do them. A true servant is one that is obedient to Me at all times. Being a true servant is to do the things that I have asked you to do because it needs to be done and to do it as you are doing for Me. It also means that you serve someone who needs it regardless if you think they deserve it. You do it because I have asked you to do it.

My Son is a true example of a true servant. He died on the cross and shed his blood so that all sinners could make it to heaven. He did not do it because you deserved it. He did it in obedience to Me. He did it because We love you that much, and We want you to be here in heaven with us and make heaven your home.

There are many things that happens during your lifetime that you have done that is not pleasing to Me or makes it where you do not deserve to have things done for you. But because of My Son, He made a way for you to be able to be forgiven as you repent for your sins. This to show you that Our love is unconditional. And you need to remember from where you came. You truly need to grasp ahold of this today, My children.

You cannot be a judge of others and be a servant as well and walk the love walk that I have called you to walk. It gives you a double mind. If you have a double mind than you are not rooted and grounded in Me and focused on Me and you will fall during this dark time. I have called you to love. You first love Me and then you love each other.

To be a true servant you must ask for My kind of love to be placed in your heart. If you ask, I will place this in your hearts. I need you to love without putting judgment on others so that as I bring in My harvest of souls. As I am bringing them in, with this renewed heart and mind, you can love them as I love them. There will be many sinners coming in that if you do not have the right mindset of a servant, it will cause you to feel that they do not deserve it, but what you forget is you did not deserve it either. For you must remember, all are sinners and have come short of My glory.

So today, My children, I am asking you to fully humble yourselves and allow Me to give you a true servants heart. Allow Me to give you a heart that will love the way the way I love and a heart that will not judge.

Repent today for not truly walking in the love walk that I have called you to walk in and for not being the true servant that I have called you to be. Ask for a renewal of the mind and heart because in this hour, you truly need this to happen, so you do not fall.

I want to bring in My harvest. I need you to be true servants and to walk the love walk I have called you to walk in so I can use you in this hour. You must understand you will not get to choose who you love. I am just asking you to love all and to be obedient to My voice and to serve as My Son served.

As you have your mind and heart renewed today, you will see how I will begin to work through you with signs, miracles, and wonders that all will know has come from Me. You will then be able to radiate My love and bring the lost souls to Me and watch them be saved just as I have saved you.

Philippians 2:1-15; Luke 10:27; Matthew 7:1-2; 1 Peter 4:7-11
****

DESIRE FRIENDSHIP AND COMPANIONSHIP WITH ME

Today, My children, I want you to build a solid friendship and companionship with Me. I desire for you to talk to Me and share not just your troubles with Me, but your joys. I do not want to be remembered just in your sorrows, but also in your celebrations. I want you to build a relationship with Me that you will talk to Me just to talk to Me. I desire to do the same with you.

As you would stop to talk to a friend who calls you on the phone just to talk, I want you to do the same with Me. I want you to open your communication line with Me in a broader way today. I want you to be open to My voice at all times and in all hours of your day. I want to spend time with you in the good and the bad. I want to laugh with you as well as cry with you. I desire to travel with you as you go about your daily routines of shopping or cleaning and hear your conversation to Me.

I desire for you to just talk to Me just because you want to talk. Let Me be your sounding board. Let Me be the one who you come to first. Yes, I know that you also need a companion, a friend here on Earth. I see and understand this. It is one reason why I gave Adam, Eve. I do not desire for you to be alone while you do your works for Me and while you are on Earth. I just do not want you to forget that I am also here.

I would so desire you to just call out to Me just to sit in My presence. I desire you to call on Me just because you miss me, long to talk to me, and enjoy being with Me. I desire you to call Me your friend.

Many of you on call on Me when you are upset, angry, want Me to fix things, and need something, just as most children do with their parents. But I am more than just your Father. I desire to spend time with you. Just you and I sitting together and just talking about the funny things that brings you joy. I am a God who loves to laugh and enjoys to see My people happy and joyful, and I desire to share it with you.

116

A very few of you do this and have this relationship with Me. And to those I am asking you to teach others how to have this friendship with Me. I am asking you to bring others to Me the way that you fellowship with Me.

As you build your friendship with Me, you will see you will not feel so alone anymore. You will not have as much trouble having faith. You will not become so weary in well doing. You will find that obedience will become easier. You will find that you will be able to trust Me in a stronger way and with much less hesitation.

So I am asking you this day My children to build your friendship with Me stronger and go further in your walk with Me. Spend time with Me and share all of your life with Me. Learn how much I truly do love to hear from you. I am waiting to hear from you this day. I am waiting for you to decide to have this friendship with Me. I truly do love you, My children, and I am asking you to build this friendship with Me.

John 15:9-17; Proverbs 13:20; Job 29:2-6;
Act 17:24-28; Psalms 16:5-11
****

WALK IN UNITY WITH ME

My children, today, I want you to realize that your walk with Me needs to be a walk of unity with Me. You need to understand that as I ask you to put on the mind of My Son, to allow you to feel My heart, and to live with the Holy Spirit inside of you, that I am asking you to become united with Me.

I have asked you over and over to allow Me to conform your thoughts as My thoughts and your ways as My ways. You can only do that as you allow Me to bring unity with Me into your life every day.

My Son came to the earth to show you how to do this. Him and I are one just as you and I should be one. He walked with Me at all times. He allowed Me to be one with Him and do My works through Him. We did this because we love you. We did this because we want you to know that you do not have to go about this walk back to Me and your place here in heaven alone.

As you and I become one, you will begin to understand more of My Spirit and of Me. You will then start to see the supernatural take place. You will then begin to be the vessel of honor, a complete servant sold out to Me that I can use without hinderance or without you hesitating.

Don't you understand that I desire you to be one with Me so I can work through you to bring the lost souls into My kingdom? You have been taught so many times this, yet you still don't quite grasp what I am trying to teach you.

I need you today to understand this and walk in it. Just as I am one with My Son and one with the Holy Spirit, we work together to accomplish what needs to be done to bring you back to your place with Me. As we are one so should you be with us as well.

As you start to walk in unity with Me, things of this world will no longer be as hard as what it seems to be. As you start to walk in complete unity with Me the things that are coming will not affect you because you will truly know who you are in Me and trust that all is well no matter what is going on around you.

As you are in unity with Me, I am also asking you to be in unity with others. As you come together in unity with Me with others that are also in unity with Me many things will start to happen in your lives and in the lives of others. I will then be able to do so much more inside the church to where the drawling of My Spirit will be so strong that the souls will just start flowing in.

The enemy knows that unity is such a powerful thing. This is why he fights so hard to destroy it. Learn of being in unity with Me this day and you will see how to defeat the enemy in this area and how effective it will be to be in unity with others. You will then understand so many things that have gone on around you because of what the enemy has cause to stop the unity from taking place.

Come into unity with Me and then with others that are coming into unity with Me or are in unity with Me this day. There are a few around you who does this already and use them as an example and allow them to teach you to do this. But first come to Me and ask Me to begin this work in your life. Ask Me to make you one with Me as My Son was one with Me as He walked this earth. You will begin to see things start to make sense and unfold in your life.

Do not allow the enemy to have any more control in this area of your life. Do not allow the enemy to keep you blinded in this area any more. I am handing you this tool this day and it is up to you what you do with it.

John 17:20-23; Matthew 28:19; 1 Corinthians 1:10;
1 Corinthians 12:24-26; Colossians 3:14
****

SEASONS HAVE CHANGED

My children, today I want you to know the season has truly changed. I want you to know that you, My faithful children, you are going to reap your blessings as you continue to do the things that I have called you to do. It is harvest time for your blessings to come forth. You are now going to see the things that I have said that was going to come to pass surely come to pass.

Now I need you to understand My faithful children that some of My children did not listen to My voice and has gone astray. They did not heed to what I have told them to do, and they will now fall into a season of judgment because of disobedience. They will have to pay a price for that and carry out the sentence that I will give them individually based on what I see is just and right and what may turn their hearts back full to Me.

Do not grieve for them for they have had their chance. And they had many of warnings. I do want you to instead rejoice for you will start to see the fruits of your labor. I want you to know that all you have done in obedience will be rewarded and now is the season to reap the harvest that is waiting for you.

Now not only is it harvest time for your blessings, but it is also harvest time for bringing in the lost souls. There is going to be much changing going on in My church so that this will be able to come forth as I have ordained it to.

My faithful children, you must understand that I am doing these works in you as you allow Me to do them because I need you to be completely prepared to face what is coming very soon, but also to be able to not allow it to affect you as you are ministering to these souls.

Many of My children are narrowed minded and some are too loose minded. I need all My children to be totally focus on Me and what mind I want you to have. Very few of My faithful children have been able to do this. You need to understand this today, My children. For many changes are coming and you must be listening to My voice to know and understand when I am moving and when I am not.

You must be aware at all times what is going on around you and when to say something and when to let it go. You will need to know when to stay and when to move. I move many ways with many different people but you must understand that the enemy will do whatever it takes to try to stop Me because he knows his time is almost up. He will try to deafen My children's ears and hearts to My voice and try to cause you confusion.

He also knows that I am getting ready to move mightier than ever and his work load to destroy will become harder. The enemy will use whoever he can, and he can do it very quick and very slick. He is a trespasser and will stop at nothing to discourage you and try to get you to take your eyes off of Me. Do not allow him to do this.

You must allow Me to give you the mind of My Son for as you do this you will also have the mind of Me for My Son and I, we are one. As you do this you will be more open to the changes that I am doing and have a full understand of what is really going on at all times.

My faithful ones, you must understand that the enemy is going to keep trying to come after you even harder than ever to steal what I am giving you. He also knows that what I will be giving you will make you stronger in Me and your faith will sorrow even higher which will allow Me to continue to bring you higher in Me, and what you will do to his kingdom through Me and what I am teaching you and giving to you.

Come into My heavenly place. Come into the third heavens with Me where anything that he tries to do will not affect you.

The season of My movement is now. I am asking you My faithful children today to get prepared for this movement. Get into the spirit of celebrating and rejoicing for I am God. I am going to do all that I have promised. I am going to move in a way that you have never seen before and I desire that you get yourself in order with Me so that I can use you in this hour.

I need you to get your mind totally focused on Me. I need you to put all your trust in Me that I will take care of you through all that is here and will be coming as you do the works that I have called you to do.

Get yourselves prepared My children. Get your hearts praising, singing, worshiping, and celebrating for this is truly the season to collect the harvest of blessing that I have promised you and with that the harvest of souls are going to flow in like you never would have imagined. I want to begin the radical and supernatural changes.

So dance My faithful children. Be joyful in Me. Find your peace in Me. Enjoy what I am doing with you Continue to be prepared for all that is coming, but know that I am here directing and guiding you. Keep your faith strong and your expectations high. For this truly is harvest time!

Ecclesiastes 3; Daniel 2:20-23; 2 Corinthians 4:13-15
****

BE THANKFUL

Today, My children, I want you to be thankful and full of praise for the changes that are taking place in your lives. I have begun many works inside of you and I will continue the works.

The time of supernatural things and radical change is here and now. I have begun to bring My anointing in a little stronger as you continue to ask for it so that the intensity of all My anointing surrounding you and in you will allow you to still be able to function and do what I have called you to do.

I want you to enjoy this experience that I am giving you. I want you to be able to receive all that I have for you and be able to know what is happening to you. I also want you to be able to ask for what I want to give you. I want you to have the choice to choose if you want what I have for you.

I want you to be full of excitement of the changing of the seasons and knowing that you are receiving all that I have for you. I am preparing you be able to contain, keep, and to be grateful for all that I am doing for you. I want you to be able to hold onto all that I am doing and not allow the enemy to steal it again like he has done in the past. I want you to have the fight inside of you that you will not let the enemy take not one piece of the blessings and anointing that I am giving you.

Harvest time is a happy and joyful time. It is a time to gather all that I have been preparing you for. It is a time where your joy will be watered and replenished from its dormant state. I want to give you even more joy then you have ever had. With this joy, will come much strength, and you will be able to use it to defeat the enemy of your soul.

I want you to give thanks to Me for all that I have already done, I am doing, and all that I am going to do. I want your heart to be so full of thankfulness that as you receive all that I have for you that you will want to go out and testify to all those around you of just how good I am to you. I want you to use your testimonies to bring in the harvest of souls that I am bringing into My church.

I want you to get into your spirit that all is well. Do not allow the enemy to use your circumstances against you any longer. Do not allow the enemy to whisper lies of deception or of false accusations anymore. Do not allow the enemy to take away your hope, faith, and expectancy away from you any longer.
\
You stop the enemy by singing praise of thankfulness to Me about all the things that are taking place. You need to allow the joy to be bubble up inside of you. You need to realize that you can come up into the heavenly and rise above all that the things that the enemy has tried and will continue to try to do. The enemy cannot stand to hear you be thankful or to hear you praise Me.

Allow your heart to be overflowing this day with lots of praise and thankfulness of the things that is happen in the now and in the future. For the things of the past will not be able to be compared to what I am going to do with you and for you in the very short days ahead.

Allow singing to come from your lips today of praises. Oh how I love to hear your praises. I love to hear the songs of your heart. As you sing your praises today, you will feel the joy start rising inside of you and the more you sing today the stronger your joy will become and the stronger you will become in Me.

Study My Word and see just what praise has brought to My people. See what just praising Me has help them through and how they defeated many enemies. For I want you to understand that with your praises you will be able to use it to protect your blessings and anointing from the enemy.

With your praises you will be able to defeat the enemy every time he tries to peak up his head. With praises you will be able to endure all that is coming and that you will see it will not affect you. For in your praises you will then become to know that I am a God who will always provide, will always be by your side, and I truly do love you and I will protect you.

Today is your day to praise and be thankful and just know with all that is in you that the seasons have changed. Celebrate for it is the time of the harvest of blessings, anointings, gifts, signs, miracles, and wonders, and most of all time to bring in My lost children back to My arms and to the cross so that they may be saved.

Hebrews 12: 1-3; 2 Chronicles 5:12-14; Psalms 50:14-15; Psalms 100; Colossians 3:16; Psalms 71:8

****

PRESS INTO WORSHIP

Today, My children, I want you to really press into your worship to Me today. I want you to really open up your hearts to Me. I want you to pour out all that you feel, all that you have desire of, and just how much you really do love Me.

I love to hear you worship, My children. I love when you open your hearts to Me. I love when you desire to really feel My presence with you. I am always with you, but as you worship you invite Me there with you, to move in more ways that I want to move because you become more open to Me.

I want you to come into a higher level with Me today. I desire for you to come up to the throne room of My grace. I want you to come into the Holy of Holies and really enter in My presence. The sounds of your worship are such a sweet sound to My ears and a delight in My heart. As you worship many things will really begin to take place in you and new songs of worship will take place inside of you and through you.

I want you to really press into all that I have for you this day. There is so much I want to give you, My children. Oh how I desire to hear the songs of your hearts. As you truly press into your worship today to Me, you will see Me move in a mightier way than you have ever seen Me more before.

As you worship Me, I will meet you and bring you into that higher place that you so long to be in. I want to complete the works that you have allowed Me to begin inside of you. I want to finish the transitioning and renewing of yourselves in Me that you have been going through.

I see the hearts of My people, but today I desire to hear your hearts just pour out your lips in worship. I want to hear how much you truly love Me. I want to hear how you desire to see, know, and feel Me even more into your lives. As you press into true worship today your joy will increase more than you have ever felt it before. You will enter a peace that you have only begun to experience. Your faith and trust will begin to really sore higher in Me.

The breakthroughs that you need in your lives will be achieved as you worship Me. There are still things hidden in your hearts and in your lives that needs to be taken care of. As you worship Me this day, I will remove these things. I will mend the things that are broken or have become unraveled. As you worship Me, I will do things that you are not even aware needs to be done. A change will take place that you are so longing for.

If you really press into your worship to Me, I will reveal many things to you. If you really press into your worship with Me I will show you a taste of just how powerful it really is. I will begin to place a new understanding and wisdom inside of you that you have been asking for. I will increase your knowledge of Me as you truly worship Me this day.

I will meet you today in your worship with Me. I do not care where you begin your worship to Me. I will be there. Just let your worship, true worship begin. Allow your heart to open up and just pour out from your lips of just how much you love and worship Me. Sing and worship from your heart though your lips of how much you desire to have Me with you.

If you worship Me in your car, I will be there. If you worship Me in the bathroom or shower, I will be there. If you worship Me in your prayer closet, I will be there. If you worship Me as you work or play outside I will be there. Where ever you are just let your worship begin to flow from within and work itself out and just watch what I will do for and in you today.

This is what I desire from you today. Will you come to Me and really press into your worship to Me and open up your hearts? Will you come to Me in true worship and allow your lips to sing new songs to Me of just how much you love Me and desire Me in your hearts?

I desire for you to truly feel more of My presence and to spend more time together this day. I really desire to hear your worship from your heart and lips today. As you really press into your worship, really open up yourself and allow the walls to come down from your heart. Allow yourself to come higher in Me. You will see what I will do for you and to you today as you press into true worship to Me.

John 4:24; Hebrews 13:15; Psalms 40:3; Colossians 3:14-17;
Hebrews 12:28-29; Psalms 95:6-7

****

CELEBRATE IN UNITY

Today, My children, I want you to celebrate in My presence with one another. I want you to praise Me from the depths of your hearts. I want you to come together in unity, in the same mindset and same goal to come into My house to praise Me. I want you to come into My presence today expecting all that I have for you; and for Me to move in a mighty way.

I want you to come together in fellowship and full of joy. As you come together to celebrate together in My name and in My presence, do so in My glory and with much encouragement to one another. Share together all that I have done for you and what you believe for Me to do for you in the future.

If one of you are down and full of sadness, lift that one up and show them just how good I am. Give them words full of life in Me. Bring much of My joy to their lives so that I can rebirth My joy in them. If one of you are feeling unloved and not worthy, let My love radiate from you that they will feel what it is to be loved and to share with them that they are loved, for I love all of My children.

Today, My children, has been ordained to share with one another all the things that I have done for you. Today is the day that I want you to lift up, encourage, celebrate, and be merry in My presence and with one another. As you do this a stronger unity will begin to grow and seeds will be planted to make My body stronger for all the challenges that lies ahead.

Today is the day that much laughter, joy, hope, and strength will be on your lips and flowing from your hearts to one another as you come together in My honor and share your testimonies with each other building and lifting up those who need it. As you do this you are training for what is expected of you as My lost souls come into My house. You will be more open to share with them as you do with each other.

So today, I want you to come into My house, celebrate in My name, come together and encourage one another. Share your blessings with one another, build up and edify My name. For I am your God and you are My children.

As you come together, do so to My glory and My honor, and I will be there with you. Let the joy and love bubble up inside of you like never before and let it flow out of you for all to see how great I am to you. Let all see that I am your God; and I want to see My children happy.

Acts 2:42-47; 1 Corinthians 10:31; 1 Thessalonians 5:11;
Hebrews 10:25; Colossians 3:16
****

SHOWERING BLESSINGS

Today, My children, I want you to know that I have begun the showers of My blessings upon My children. I have given you, My children, promises of things that I want to do for you and now is the time to receive them. But I want you to know that you must not have your umbrella up to stop the blessings from raining on you.

Some of you My children are not still yielding to all of what I have told you to do and being obedient to My voice. You still want to hold on to a little control for yourself.

I am letting you know today that this will block some of the blessings I have for you. I am asking you to completely let go of all of the worldly things that stops you from 100% following and serving Me. I need you to lay down all those things that so easily turns your head and ears away from Me even for a split second and just give all of yourself to Me.

I need to have all of you so that as your blessings come the enemy will not be able to use what you have been given from Me against you or take it away from you. The enemy knows that if you receive all that I have promised you that your walk will become stronger in Me because most of you that I have promised blessings to will be able to use them to testify what I have done in your life. The enemy only comes to steal, kill, and destroy and you must remember and understand this.

Disobedience to My voice and calling will stop you from receiving the blessings that I have from you. You cannot any longer dilly dally in the things that I have asked you to do. I need you to get before Me this day and search your hearts and make sure that you have done what I have asked you to do to receive your blessings. If you have not done them, you must do them now and quickly.

This is the time for your callings to come forth. This is the time to allow My anointing to flow through you at all times and bring in My harvest of souls as I give you the harvest of blessings. This is the time that I desire to use all of My children. Do not hesitate from doing what I have called you to do. There is no more time to question if you want to do it or not. I need My children to be a "YES" child.

The heavens are open and have begun to shower the blessings on you that you have been waiting for. As you receive the blessings use them wisely and to My honor and glory.

Some of you will be given the small things first to see how you will handle them and use them for My kingdom before I pour out the bigger ones.

Some of you, My children, still have to wait for certain things to happen because I need you where you are at. Please do not get discouraged and dismayed. Know that I am doing and giving you all the blessing I have promised.

Some of you, My children, will receive things very quickly and I want you to remember all that I am giving you and use it to encourage others to keep pressing forward and use the gifts to further My kingdom.

You are My children and I am your Father. I am your God and I do not lie. I desire to give you all that I said I would give you but you must be obedient to My voice and have sold out to Me. The showers have begun and all will begin to come forth just as I said they would. Do not block these blessings with umbrellas of disobedience or lack of surrendering your all.

Celebrate today knowing that your blessings are here. And make sure that you have lined up according to what I have already told you to do and make sure that you are not holding on to any of the worldly ways that would stop you from receiving all that I have for you.

I am your Father, My children, and I want to shower you with all the gifts and blessings and promises just as I did Abraham, Issac, and Jacob because I truly love you. I want My children to see and know just what kind of Father I really am and be able to tell those who are lost all about what your Father has done for you. Search yourselves this day, put away the umbrellas, and open yourselves to receive all that I have for you.

Isaiah 1:19; Joshua 21:45; I Kings 8:56-61

****

www.ingramcontent.com/pod-product-compliance
Lightning Source LLC
Chambersburg PA
CBHW061737020426
42331CB00006B/1265